D1194681

CARLO GIORDANO - ISIDORO KAHN

THE JEWS

in

POMPEII, HERCULANEUM, STABIAE

and in the Cities of Campania Felix

(English translation by Wilhelmina F. Jashemski)

Third Etition

(Rev. and enlarged by Laurentino García y García)

BARDI EDITORE

In the cover: Drawing with the Magic Square «Sator-Rotas».

Seconda ristampa febbraio 2006

© 2001 BARDI EDITORE s.r.l.
Via Piave, 7 – 00187 Roma
ISBN 88-85699-91-X

*To the Jewish victims
of the eruption of 79 C.E.
in the 19° centennial.*

PREFACE TO THE SECOND AND THIRD EDITIONS

On August 24, 1979, one thousand and nine hundred years will have passed since the towns of Pompeii, Herculaneum and Stabiae were crushed and covered by Mt. Vesuvius, whose cruel indifference to human suffering was celebrated in a famous lyric, *The Broom-flower*, by the famous 19th century poet, Giacomo Leopardi.

In the course of his poem, he images the oblivion of the dead ruins being broken only by the rare visits of occasional wanderers. Today, instead, they are vivified by the presence of numerous scholars for whom they constitute a mine of information; artists from near and far come to study and to learn and crowds of visitors arrive daily to find spiritual comfort in meditating on the past – a respite hard to come by nowadays.

In order to commemorate this occasion, the authors and publisher have decided to issue a second edition (and now a third reprint) of the book: *The Jews in Pompeii Herculaneum Stabiae and in the cities of Campania Felix.*

There are two other reasons for this decision as well: the first is that we owe the oldest classical evidence of the eruption of 79 c.e. and the burial of the three towns to the hand of an ancient Jewish author. It is a passage from the IV book of the *Libri Sibillini* written by an anonymous Jew, who sees the catastrophe of the Vesuvian towns as one of the many punishments deriving from the destruction of Jerusalem and from the evil done «to the pious men who lived around Solomon's Temple». His testimony of the tragic eruption was composed only a year after it took place, no later than August of the year 80. By contrast, Martial's famous verses were written in 88 and the two letters by Pliny the Younger, an eye witness to the event, are dated respectively 106 and 107.

If the Hebrew word «cherem « found a few years ago, together with the two Stars of Solomon, has among its different meanings that of vineyard, let us formulate a sincere wish that the three Vesuvian cities, once obliterated and now brought back to light of day, be a prosperous «cherem «, a flourishing Vineyard, from which scholars, artists and people with sensitivity may draw abundantly.

It is our utmost desire that future visitors upon departing may wish to return soon to renew their enchantment.

With Goethe on his Italian Journey, we can still repeat: «Halt your flight, o instant, thou art so fair!».

CHAPTER I

THE JEWS IN ITALY BEFORE 79 C. E.

The story of the Jews in Italy is one of the most interesting chapters in the history of the people of Israel in exile. The
little information we possess contains discrepancies regarding
the precise period in which the Jews were established on
Italian soil, but it is certain that even before the destruction of
the Temple at Jerusalem by Titus, numerous Jews were already living in Rome, in the neighbourhood of Naples, and in
various others localities in the southern part of the peninsula.

The Jewish emigration to the Occident began properly,
as is known, with the conquest of Judaea by Alexander the
Great, who, in order to give a durable foundation to his empire, encouraged and favoured the meeting and fusion of the
conquered population and the victors. Thus in addition to
those in Babylonia, Egypt (1) and North Africa, other
Jewish colonies arose along the coast of the Mediterranean
and in the Greek Archipelago. In the works of the Jewish
historian Flavius Josephus (2) who lived in the first century
C.E., we also find evidence of the settling of the Jews in
Antioch, Phoenicia, and the regions of Phrygia and Lydia.

The Jews next directed their steps to Italy, and especially
to Rome, which was beginning at this time to become the cen-

---

(1) There was considerable Jewish emigration to Alexandria of Egypt, from
the first years of its founding. See Josephus Flavius, *Bellum Judaicum*, 2. 487.499.
On the extent of the Jews in the Diaspora long before Titus destroyed Jerusalem,
among other scholars see especially J. Juster, *Les juifs dans l'empire romaine*,
Paris 1914, vol.1, pp.179-212; C. Roth, *Short History of the Jewish People*,
London 1935, pp.140-150.

(2) Josephus Flavius, *Antiquitates Judaicae*, 12. 119-120; *Contra Apionem*, 1.
194-214. All references to Josephus are given by books and sections as shown in
the English text of M. A. Thackeray, *Josephus* – with an English translation – in
nine volumes, London 1961-1965. Hereafter the works abbreviated as: *Bellum
Judaicum, B.J.; Antiquates Judaicae, A.J.; Contra Apionem, C.A.*

tre of all the migratory streams. It has been correctly said however that at Rome the Jews appeared relatively later than elsewhere. It should not be forgotten that until their conquest of the Mediterranean world, the Romans considered themselves essentiality an agricultural people, more inclined to support a nationalism of the type favoured by Cato the Censor, a nationalism which combined with love of the land, little liking for the sea and for the stranger, especially for the Greek and Oriental merchants (3). For this reason, the Jews, at least at first, were attracted largely to the more active and more open commercial centres of the Mediterranean world. Comparatively few chose as their new home the city of Rome. But with the new policy of the Capitol, Rome became more cosmopolitan and offered to foreigners multiple advantages and guarantees of religious liberty. Thus numerous Jews, having disembarked at the port of Brindisi and made their way to Pozzuoli, through Apulia, Samnium, and Campania some getting as far as Rome others settling along the way.

In the new environment the Jews did not delay organizing themselves in a better manner. But however distant they were, and although constituting an ethnic minority, they never forgot the motherland and the need to help brothers in misfortune. When the victorious Roman legions brought back Jewish prisoners, their co-religionists ransomed them, if they had not already been freed by the masters themselves who found Jewish slaves of little use because of their fierce intransigence in observing the prescribed Sabbath and their dietary laws (4). Thus many of the freed prisoners with their descendants assumed the condition of freedmen, and did not hesitate to mix with the Roman plebeian and to live in the most crowded quarters of Rome (5), a social phenomenon that one observes also at Pompeii.

(3) H. J. Leon, *The Jews of Ancient*, Philadelphia 1960, p.2.
(4) *ibid., 4.*
(5) In all probability the first Jewish settlement at Rome was in the crowded region of Trastevere (Transtiberium area), where the poor lived, but gradually Jews moved into many other quarters of the city. There were also important Jewish colonies in Ostia and Portus. In the spring of 1961, during work on the

According to Valerius Maximus *(De superstitionibus* 1. 3, 3) they did not concern themselves only with their trade, but also with proselytising. He tells us that in 139 B. C. E., probably while the third Hasmonean Embassy sent by Simon Maccabeus (6) as at Rome, Gnaeus Cornelius Hispanus compelled the Jews to return immediately to their own countries, accusing them of contaminating the morals of Rome with the cult of Jove Sabatio (7).

During the last century of the Republic the number of Jews in Italy increased considerably, especially with the prisoners of war that Gnaeus Pompeius brought back in 61 B. C.E. after the conquest of Judaea for his triumphal return to Rome. Within a few years, moreover, these Jews attained such solid positions that from that moment their influence was actively felt in the political life of the time.

A passage in Cicero *(Pro Flaco 66-68)* tells us of the political line followed by the Jews during the last years of the Republic. In fact, on the occasion of the suit brought by L. Valerius Flaccus, accused of unlawful appropriation, of arbitrary confiscation and illegal possession of gold collected from the Jews for the Temple at Jerusalem, the great orator of Arpinum, in defending his client, accused the Jews of plotting against every good Roman *(in optimum quemque).* Now in the use of such a phrase, it is easy to discern the reference to those of his own party, because the members of the conservative senatorial group of which Cicero was the leader were called *optimates.* The Jews, therefore, deduced

construction of the road to Fiumicino Airport, in the vicinity of ancient Ostia, the remains of ancient synagogue came to light-perhaps the oldest in Europe. According to Professor Maria Floriani Squarciapino *(Ebrei a Roma e ad Ostia,* in: Studi Romani vol. 11, 1963, n. 2, pp. 129-141) the remains found are unquestionably of the fourth century C. E., but this synagogue stood upon an earlier one of different plan that had been built in the first century.

(6) For the identification of the Hasmonean Embassy see G. Ricciotti, *Storia d'Israele,* Turin, 1960, vol. 2, p. 325.

(7) The report of the Latin historian and writer is very obscure. But it appears evident that the drastic provision was directed only against part of the Jewish community at Rome, presumably against foreign Jewish merchants who had been in Rome only a short time. See Th. Reinach, *Textes d'auteurs grecs et romains relatifs au Judaisme,* Paris 1895, p. 239.

from the stinging, calumnious tone of the great orator, that they ought to take sides with the *populares,* the democratic party of which young Caesar was the favourite leader. They effectively sided with him in the civil war of 49 B. C. E.

In recognition of the aid received, Caesar showed himself well disposed toward the Israelites, and gave them privileges, which, recognized down to the period of the Christian emperors, have been called the «Magna Charta» of the Jews. These privileges included freedom of worship, authorization to constitute a community, freedom from military service, and the right to judge their suits according to Jewish law (8),

It was also in this period, with the advent of the Mystery religions in Italy, that the work of Jewish proselytising in the cultured classes of the *gens Romana* gained momentum. Jewish thought even made its influence felt in Latin poetry. In fact, according to recent literary views, the Messianic hope of a better world (echoing Old Testament hopes) found in the Fourth Eclogue of Virgil, and dedicated by him to the consul Pollio, was perhaps due to the personal friendship between Herod and Pollio (9).

But that sentiment of broad, liberal thought, which was shaping the political conduct of Rome in those years in respect to her population and to the Jewish world, suffered a serious setback under Tiberius. The restrictive orders emanating from that emperor in 19 C. E., were probably suggested by Sejanus, the extremely bitter, anti-Semitic minister of Tiberius. The Roman Senate decreed the expulsion of the Jews from all Italy (10). At the same time their sacred utensils and manuscripts were seized and given to the flames. About four thousand Jews who were residing in Rome with their families were led away from their homes and deported to Sardinia (Josephus *A.J.*, 18. 84; Tacitus *Annales 2.* 85 ff.),

(8) Juster, *op. cit.*, vol. 2, p. 110.
(9) Josephus Flavius, *A.J.,* 14. 138 L. H. Feldman, *Asinius Pollio and his Jewish Interests,* in: Transactions of the American Philological Association vol.84, 1953, pp.73-80. For the influence of Jewish thought on Vergil see E. Paratore, *Storia della letteratura latina,* Florence 1961, p. 359.
(10) Leon, *op. cit.*, p. 18 ff.

then inhospitable and dangerous because of the numerous brigands who were infesting it and because of its unhealthy climate (11). At the fall of Sejanus, Tiberius confirmed the privileges formerly conceded by Caesar and by Augustus, and the Jews were able to return to Rome.

During the reign of Claudius other episodes of intolerance took place, and pictorial documents at Pompeii from this time show that such sentiments were shared by some inhabitants of the Campanian cities. Such acts come out in the edict of expulsion, the reason for which is indicated by Suetonius (*Claudius* 25) in his celebrated passage: *Iudaeos impulsore Chresto assidue tumultuantes Roma expulit.* The passage from the Latin historian is very brief and certainly not entirely clear, but it is evident that some altercations broke out among the Jews. Today it is almost unanimously agreed by all historians that very probably this *Chrestus,* cause of the Jewish tumults, was Jesus of Nazareth (12).

There were then at Rome, in the bosom of the Jewish community, two parties, in violent opposition to each other, one made up of those who saw in Jesus the expected Messiah, and another made up of those who denied such identification (13). It is interesting, in this respect, to note that at Pompeii the first evidence of nascent Christianity was discovered in a place in which probable Jewish traces were found. And the evidence was of a polemic nature.

The expulsion threatened by Claudius did not even take place. But some of the more conspicuous Jews and some most compromised by the new faith, were banished from Rome, or at least they preferred to go away. Among these were Aquila and Priscilla who settled in Corinth and with whom Paul of Tarsus stayed; later when Paul came to

(11) Any traces of Hebrew language or Jewish customs in Sardinia today are probably due to this Jewish colony. See A. Milano, *Storia degli Ebrei in Italia*, Turin 1963, p. 14.

(12) Ricciotti, *op. cit.,* p. 223.

(13) For the controversial passage see H. Janne, *Impulsore Chresto*, in : Mélanges G. Bidez (= Annuarie de l'Institut de Philologie et d'Histoire Orientales 2), 1934, pp. 531-535 and Leon, *op. cit.*, p. 27.

Pozzuoli, he was entertained by a group of Jews for seven days (*I Corinthians* 16.191; *Acts* 18.1; 28.13).

The years of Nero's reign passed tranquilly for the Jews of the Empire. One recalls that Poppea Sabina, according to some of Pompeian birth, and certainly of Pompeian family name, having become the wife of Nero, followed an enthusiastic political course in favour of the Jews. We do not know in what measure the Campanian Jewish environment influenced the sentiments of the Empress, but it is certain that if not actually converted she at least followed very closely monotheistic thought and religious practices. The Jewish historian Josephus (*A.J.*, 20.195) calls her a «God fearing woman». Moreover, the same Josephus, having come to Rome, was presented to the Empress by the Jewish actor Alityro, a favourite of Nero, and he was aided by her in his petitions to the Emperor (14).

The fall of Jerusalem, although it did not abolish the privileges conceded to the Jews, had grave repercussions for the Jewish population of the Empire. The tax of two drachmas, which up to that time had been paid by the Jews for the maintenance of the Temple in Jerusalem, was assigned, with the naming of the *fiscus judaicus,* to the Capitoline Temple, and was paid to the *Procurator and capitularia Judeorum* (15) for the imperial fisc. In such a way Vespasian intended to restore, with the money taken from the Jews, the public treasury exhausted by the extravagance of Nero, and by the warlike ambitions of his successors. This tax continued to be imposed on the Jews (16) for the next three centuries, even by Christian emperors, and was abolished in 361 by Julian the Apostate.

The end of the Jewish war caused a large increase in the Jewish population of Italy. Tens of thousands of prisoners

---

(14) For Poppea Sabina in Pompeii see M. Della Corte, *Case ed abitanti in Pompei*, 2. ed., Pompei 1954, p.58. On the Judaizing of Poppea see B. W. Henderson, *Life and Principate of the Emperor Nero*, London 1903, p.467.

(15) *Corpus Inscriptionum Latinarum*, VI, 8604. Hereafter cited as *CIL*.

(16) See Milano, *op. cit.*, p. 19; M. S. Ginsburg, *Fiscus Judaicus*, in: Jewish Quarterly Review vol. 21, 1931, p. 281. The tax resulted in the compilation of a list in which the names of the taxed Jews were registered.

were carried in part to Rome and in part to South Italy. But by now the tragedy of the Vesuvian countryside was at hand! The terrible cataclysm was understood and this was true also of the sudden and immature death of Titus – as a deserved punishment for the destruction of the Sanctuary at Jerusalem (17).

Dark omens had a little before greatly disturbed the people. Among the signs interpreted as presaging bad luck was the comet which was said to have tracked the southern heavens for six months, from the autumn of 60 C. E. to the spring of 61. And actually a year later, on February 1, 62, a great earthquake devastated the southern part of Campania.

To the creation of this gloomy atmosphere of an imminent catastrophe of the Roman world, the Jewish spirit, which could not be broken by Roman domination, along with the prophetic visions of the Apocalypse and the book of Enoch (18) contributed not a little. The vision of a land in the west smoking with fire, near to a mountain from which came streams of gold, silver, iron and lead mixed together, and with boiling waters which served to heal the illnesses of the body and the vices of luxury, corresponds undoubtedly to the Phlegraean Fields and islands which had struck the imagination of the Biblical writers, just as the crater of Solfatara, the waters and boiling vapours of Baiae, and the legends of gold and other metals flowing in the veins of Epomeo, on the island of Ischia, had entered the fantasy of the first Greek navigators.

And again in the fourth book of the Sibylline Oracle, written presumably in a Jewish environment, the unknown author predicted that a little time after the fall of Judaea, fire from the bosom of the earth would be flung into the infinite space of the heavens, falling in the form of a rain of fire on many cities of Italy. In such a manner divine punishment was

---

(17) See *The Universal Jewish Encyclopaedia*, 10 vols., New York 1939-43, s. v. «Titus».

(18) A. Maiuri, *La Campania al tempo dell'approdo di San Paolo*, Sorrento – Napoli 1991, p.15.

manifestly seen to follow the slaughter of the nation of pious men who stayed within the Sanctuary of Jerusalem (19). And in the same way that the Jewish spirit had experienced, with the tragic loss of national liberty, the truthfulness of the prophetic words which foretold the destruction of the house of Israel, so the Jews saw in the Sibylline Oracle the unconscious revelation of the divine will which punished human wickedness in the destruction of that Sacred Temple, which, built by King Solomon, had been dedicated to the God of all peoples *(I Kings* 8. 41).

It was also on Campanian land and on the burnt shore of Pompeii that for the first time the idea of the God of Sodom and Gomorrah, avenger of human wickedness in the midst of fire, was reflected in the early Christian belief that God, as censor, did not allow the abrogation of his justice. As Tertullian *(De palio* 2) has said, because of the impiety of their inhabitants, both Volsini in *Tuscia* (Tuscany), and Pompeii in Campania were deservedly destroyed by a rain of fire.

(19) The fourth book of the Sibylline Oracle according to some scholars was composed about 80 C. E. It would contain then the earliest account of the destruction of Pompeii, earlier than that of Martial (4, 44) written in 88, or that of Pliny written in 106-107. On this see A. Sogliano, *Di un luogo dei libri sibillini...*, in: Atti dell'Accademia di Archeol. Lettere e BB.AA. di Napoli vol.16 (1891-93), Napoli 1894, Parte prima, p.165; Arnold, *Die Neronische Cristenverfolgung*, Leipzig 1888, p. 80 ff.

Fig. 1. Pompeii, House of Pansa, Wiew of Vesuvius

CHAPTER II

THE JEWS IN CAMPANIA FELIX

The traces of the Jews in southern Italy at least for the first two centuries of the Empire are still wrapped in obscurity, especially before the fall of Jerusalem on the tenth of Loos (August 6th), 70 C. E. The most ancient document, and the most noteworthy one relating to the Jews of Apulia and Calabria, is from the time of the emperor Honorius (1), while the most ancient epitaphs from the Jewish catacombs of Venosa, as is well-known, are earlier than the third century (2). So it happens that the epigraphic evidence that has come to light in a few enchanting places which look out over the Gulf of Naples or lie comfortably at the base of Vesuvius, all from the first century C. E. or a little later, is the most ancient not only in South Italy, but in the entire peninsula.

1 – POZZUOLI

The ancient city of Pozzuoli, twelve kilometres to the west of Naples, founded by Samian fugitives, was still in the first century an important commercial centre for the trade between Rome and the Graeco-Oriental world.

(1) A remote Jewish settlement in Apulia is reported in the chronicle *Josippon* but the accounts in this chronicle are not always accurate. On *Josippon* see U. Cassuto, *Storia della letteratura ebraica postbiblica*, Florence 1938, p.123; A. Toaff, *Cronaca Ebraica del Sepher Yosephon*, 1969, Preface, pp.XIII, XXXVI.

(2) N. Tamassia, *Stranieri ed Ebrei nell'Italia meridionale*, in: Atti Accademici dell'Istituto Veneto 8, Venezia 1903-04, Tomo LXII, 2ª. parte, p.796; G. I. Ascoli, *Iscrizioni inedite o mal note, latine, greche ed ebraiche nel Napoletano*, in: Atti del IV Congresso degli Orientalisti, Florence 1880, vol.1, p. 239; L. Levi, *Ricerche di epigrafia ebraica nell'Italia meridionale*, in: Scritti in memoria di F. Luzzatto, Rassegna Mensile Israel. vol.33, Venezia1962, p. 132; J. B. Frey, *Corpus Inscriptionum Judaicarum*, Città del Vaticano 1936, vol. 1: Europe, pp.408-418. Hereafter cited as *CIJ*.

Fig. 2. Campi Flegrei. Pozzuoli and Capo Miseno.

The existence of a Jewish colony in this city in 60 C.E. has already been mentioned. It was later visited by Flavius Josephus (*A.J.*, 17. 328). But the first mention of Jews at *Puteoli* comes from 4 C. E. and we know that they continued to live there from this time (3).

Josephus informs us (*B.J.*, 2.104) of the misfortune that happened to the Jews at Pozzuoli when an impostor who pretended to be Alexander, the son of Herod, was welcomed with regal honours by his co-religionists, friends of his pretended father, and escorted with great merry-making during his passage through the city.

The Jewish colony of Pozzuoli, as is shown by some inscriptions, must have been large and strong. It must have contributed not a little to the prosperity of the town, controlling both the commercial activity, and the manufacturing of purple, fabric, and glass. The latter industry was based in the *vico vitrario* and flourished because of the ease with which the basic material could be found in the siliceous sand of the nearby Cumean shore.

(3) Josephus Flavius, *A.J.*, 5. 16.

Photo Pezzini

The epigraphic evidence from Pozzuoli is interesting, and from it we are able to get valuable details. From an inscription, found fittingly in the Marano Quarter (4), we learn that at Pozzuoli there was a *gerusia* or Council of Elders, led by a certain *T. Claudius Philippus,* who, we see, was interested in the construction of a wall (5). The text reads:

T. CLAUDIUS
PHILIPPUS
DIA VIVET
GERUSIARCHES
MACERIAM DUXIT

Another interesting inscription found on the tombstone of *Claudius Coeranus,* a merchant of iron tools, and vases for wine, came to light in 1854 and was published in the same year by Giulio Minervini (6). The text is as follows:

(4) *CIL*, X, 1893.
(5) On the *gerousiae* see Levi *op. cit.*, p.150; on the *dia vivet* (for eternal life!) see Ascoli, *op. cit.*, p.344.
(6) G. Minervini, *Bullettino Archeologico Napoletano* N. S. vol.3, Napoli 1855, (n. 57, Nov. 1854), p.53; *CIL*, X, 1931.

D. M.
P. CAULIO COERANO
NEGOTIATORI
FERRARIARUM ET
VINARIARIAE
ACIBAS LIB.
PATRONO MERENTI

It is true that Minervini in his first attempt to identify this freedman *Acibas,* who with a grateful heart recalled his old master, the deceased rich merchant, did not recognize the name as Jewish, since he at first suggested the reading *Alibas* in place of *Acibal.* But in February of the following year (7) the scholar returned to the subject, and describing his personal examination of the inscription, said that he was convinced that the name was *Acibas,* and that he accepted the inscription as Jewish evidence. He added that it probably referred to the same *Aciba,* whose name is recorded on another inscription from *Puteoli (CIL,* X, 2258) published some years before (8):

D. M.
P. CLAUDIUS ACIBA
SIBI FECIT

And lastly, a tomb inscription (9) of uncertain prove-

(7) G. Minervini, *Giudei in Pozzuoli*, Bull. Archeol. Napoletano N.S. vol.3, Napoli 1855, (n. 64, Feb. 1855), p.105.
(8) Matranga, *Bullettino dell'Instituto di corrispondenza archeologica*, Roma 1850, p.177; T. Mommsen, *Inscriptiones Regni Neapolitani latinae*, Lipsiae 1852, n. 7222. One of the most celebrated doctors of the Mishnà, who lived in the first century and the beginning of the second, had the name Aciba (Aqivà). For the life and work of this famous teacher, who according to tradition after being cruelly tortured was put to death by Hadrian, see G. B. De Rossi, *Dizionario degli autori Ebrei*, Parma 1802, p.41.
(9) *CIL*, X, 3303. The inscription is still an object of dispute; by some it is thought to be from Puteoli (Tamassia, *op. cit.,* 807), and by others probably from Salerno, from a time not before the fourth century (Frey, *CIJ*, 418). For *rebbites* understood as the plural of *rabbi* see Ascoli, *op. cit.,*p. 256. For the identification of *vinea Mazae* with the present *La Gajola* at Posillipo see N. F. Pelosini,

nance, reported as having been found at Naples in the *vinea Mazae*, is the one which commemorated the seventeen year old *Benus*, daughter of the Rabbi Abundantis:

HIC REQUIESCIT IN PACE
BENUS FILIA REBBETIS
ABUNDANTIS QUI VIXIT
ANNUS PLM XVII D. P. II ID

VII.‏הַאֲבֻנְדַּנְטִיס בְּשַׁלְוָם‏ ‏דַאֲנֹתוֹשֵׁי‏
‏לַ‏ ‏דוּר‏ ‏זְוֵעֲ‏‏נִוֹם‏

2 – NOLA

An inscription found in the Seminary at Nola and interpreted by Mommsen (10), although it is probably not before the fifth century, deserves to be mentioned here because it undoubtedly shows that Jews had for some time also made their home in this Campanian city. That this Jewish colony, rather than decreasing in size or disappearing, had on the contrary increased and become strong is proved by the authentic testimony of Uranius, who in his epistle, *De obitu Paulini ad Pacatum,* narrates how during the funeral of Paulinus, together with the Christians, numerous Jews and Pagans also followed the bier with great sorrow (11). The inscription commemorated a certain *Bonito*, son of *Staurace*:

Ricordi, tradizioni e leggende dei Monti Pisani, Pisa 1890, p.31. The Hebrew could only be interpreted: *Beshalom... Benus = In peace... Benus.*

(10) *CIL*, X, 1367. Frey *(CIJ,* 409) unreasonably supports the Christian origin of this inscription.

(11) Uranius Presbyter, *Epistula de obitu Paulini ad Pacatum* (Migne Ed.), vol. 53, col. 859.

Fig. 3. Baccoli

HIC REQUIESCIT IN SOMNO PACIS
BONITUS FILIO STAURACI DP. IVL
DIES XXV. I. V.

בי נומצוה ותדה אור

The Latin text is followed by a group of Hebrew letters which Professor Eude Lolli read as the following Biblical verse

KI NER MIZWÀ VETORÀ OR

«For the commandments are a lamp and the Law is light» (12)

(12) *Proverbs* 6. 23.

24

3 – BACOLI

The presence of Jews in Bacoli on the picturesque Bay of Pozzuoli is documented by a single inscription (13), in which is mentioned a certain *Herod* of *Ascalon,* for whose tomb, ground was acquired from the community of the *Baulani.* The text reads:

HERODES
APHRODISI F
ASCALON (e)
VIXIT ANNIS

(13) T. Mommsen, *Inscriptiones Regni Neapolitani latinae*, Lipsiae 1852, n. 2561.

25

XXXXII
LOCUM EMIT
AB ORDINE
BAULANORUM
DEMETRIUS
VILICUS

4 – MARANO

Also at Marano in Naples, on the northern slope of the Phlegraean Fields, there was a Jewish colony to which a Jewish girl from Jerusalem by the name of *Claudia Aster* (14) belonged. The inscription was already badly destroyed when it was discovered, but nevertheless it has been reconstructed as follows:

(CL) AUDIA ASTER
(H) IEROSOLYMITANA
(ca) PTIVA CURAM EGIT
(TI) CLAUDIUS AUG. LIBERTUS
(mas) CULUS ROGO VOS FAC.
(prae) TER LEGEM NE QUIS
(mi) HI TITULUM DEICIAT CU
(ra) M AGATIS VIXIT ANNIS
XXV

In the same city, an unknown Jew owned a bronze seal in the shape of a *planta pedis* (15), on which was a writing which can be read: *It-shalom = cum pace* (16). It is impossible, however, to determine the period from which this object

---

(14) *CIL*, X, 1971; J.B. Frey, *CIJ*, 410; N. Ferorelli, Gli *Ebrei nell'Italia meridionale, dall'età romana al sec. XVIII*, Torino 1915, pp.1-4; Milano, *Op. cit.*, p.27. Our interpretation of the inscription: *Claudia Aster from Jerusalem prisoner took care, J Masculus freedman of Ti. Claudius Augustus ask you so that no one ruins my inscription, beyond law take care. Lived 25 years.*

(15) Frey, *CIJ*, 410.

(16) R. Garrucci, *Storia dell'arte cristiana*, Prato 1873, vol. 6, Tav. 491, No. 15.

Fig. 4. The bronze seal with *It-shalom*

comes, for while some letters of the inscription correspond to the characters on the epitaphs from Venosa of the third and fourth centuries, others, for example the final *Mem,* seem identical to those found on the Palestinian epitaphs of the first century (17).

5 – CAPUA

The existence of a Jewish community in Capua is largely proved by an inscription found in the ancient *Villa Pellegrini.* This important inscription was given by a certain Matteo Zolillo to Clement XIV and should now be in the Museo Lateranense at Rome among the ancient Jewish inscriptions (18). The text is:

ALFIUS IUDA
ARCON ARCOSY
NAGOGUS QUI
ANN. LXX MESIB VII
DIEB X ALFIA SO
TERIS CUM Q AN

(17) «*Alphabet, The Hebrew*», in: The Universal Jewish Encyclopaedia, vol.1, p. 450.
(18) *CIL*, X, 2905. For the Jewish inscription of Frattaminore, the ancient Atella, little town about fourteen kilometres to the north-west of Naples, see Frey, *CIJ*, 409.

Fig. 5. Capua

Photo Buonanno

XXXXVIII COIUGI
INCOMPARABILI
BENEMERENTI
FECIT

This *Alfius Iuda,* as one gathers from his titles, was evidently the most illustrious and highly esteemed person in the Jewish congregation at Capua. If the inscription is interpreted correctly by Jean Juster (19) he was not only a member of the «Council of Elders», as seems to be implied by the title *archon,* but he also exercised the function of *rabbi,* and of spiritual head of his synagogue.

(19) Juster, *Les juifs dans l'empire romaine,* Paris 1914, vol.1, p.450, No. 4. For the various offices found in Hebrew Inscriptions see Leon H.J., *The Jews of Ancient Rome,* Philadelphia 1960, pp. 171-174, 186-187. Our interpretation of the inscription: *(Here lies) Alfius Iuda leader and spiritual head of the synagogue who lived 70 years, 7 months, 10 days. Alfia Soteris who lived with him 48 years set up (this stone) to her incomparable, worthy husband.*

6 – HERCULANEUM

Located a few miles to the east of Naples on the slope of Vesuvius, where it takes the shape of a promontory projecting into the Gulf of Naples, Herculaneum, unlike nearby industrial Pompeii, always remained in antiquity a small and tranquil Campanian town, a place favoured for the construction of elegant patrician villas. In this town too there were inhabitants of Jewish origin. In the House of the Lararium (*insula* V, entrance 31) epigraphic evidence records a certain

DAVID (20)

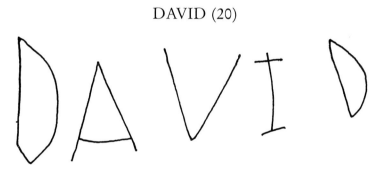

Also from some tile stamps we get the name of a servant of Livia, who was the *procurator* of her tile factory:

ABDEUS LIVIAE (21)

This name, which could be compared to that of the Jewish prophet *Obadiah* Servant of the Eternal, or to *Abdà* (*I Kings* 4.6), is a Chaldean name and also has the meaning of «servant», so for this reason it is not absolute proof of Jewish nationality.

---

(20) M. Della Corte, *Le iscrizioni di Ercolano*, in: Rendiconti dell'Accademia di Archeologia, Lettere e Belle Arti vol.33 (1958) Naples 1959, p.268.

(21) Della Corte, *Ibid*, p.283. For the presence of Jews in Herculaneum see V. Catalano, *Case, abitanti e culti in Ercolano*, in: Annali del Pontificio Istituto Superiore di Scienze e Lettere «S. Chiara» vol.13, Naples 1963, pp.307, 341 ff. – in preparation a new edition by L. García y García and G. Panzera, Rome, Bardi, 2001 –.

In Herculaneum, in the House of the Bicentennial (*insula* V), an amazing discovery was made in February 1938. After admiring the splendid marble floors and the frescoed walls of the master's quarters, the workmen continued excavating and discovered on the upper floor, in a humble room, a small wooden chest placed on a low base against the wall opposite the door. Just above the piece of furniture, which suggested a domestic altar, could be seen deeply incised into the wall, the imprint left by an object in the shape of a cross. A part of the wall around the arms of the cross, which clearly appeared to have been fastened with nails, had been whitened with plaster, as if to give it a more tidy appearance. What was the true nature of this discovery? It is not possible to say definitely, because it continues to be the centre of controversy between those who believe there were Christians at Herculaneum (22) and their opponents who refuse to recognize in this imprint the sign of the Christian cross, and evidence of this cult in Herculaneum (23).

But a later discovery, coming from the same House of the Bicentennial would seem to give substance to the theory of a famous scholar (24) who maintained that the traces of primitive Christianity at Herculaneum could be attributed to Jews attracted by the preaching of the apostle Paul. However that may be, in the rustic second floor of the house, in a room equally unadorned and humble, were found the wax tablets of a domestic archive in which were kept the transcribed actions and testimony of a trial, commonly known as the *Trial of Justa,* and still in progress at the moment of the eruption.

(22) Della Corte M., *I Cristiani a Pompei,* Rendiconti dell'Acc. di Arch. Lett. e Belle Arti di Napoli, 19 (1938-39) Napoli 1939, pp. 25-27; Maiuri A., *La croce di Ercolano,* Rendiconti della Pontificia Accad. Romana di Archeologia Ser.3 col.15 (1939) Roma 1940, pp.193-218; A. Maiuri, *Herculaneum* («Guide-books to Museums and Monuments in Italy»), Rome 1945, pp. 40-47.

(23) J Carcopino, *Études d'histoire chrétienne,* Paris 1953, pp.49-50; A. Maiuri, *Saggi di varia antichità,* Venice 1954, p.391.

(24) A. Maiuri, *La Campania al tempo dell'approdo di San Paolo,* Sorrento – Napoli 1991, p.38.

Fig. 6. Herculaneum, House of the Bicentennial

Fig. 7. The Furniture Restored

The mistress of the house, *Calatoria Temidis,* denied to *Justa,* daughter of the freedwoman *Vitalis Petronia,* the right to inherit the wealth of her dead mother. *Calatoria* maintained that the girl should be considered a slave at the time of her birth because her mother at that time had not yet been given her freedom, and that consequently as a slave the girls was not able to inherit her mother's wealth. The catastrophe kept the judges from pronouncing a wise sentence, or perhaps from committing an injustice.

But what interests us here, above all, is the name of the principal person in the trial, the freedwoman *Vitalis.* It has already been noted that the Jews in exile often changed their ethnic name to another, which in the new language had the same meaning or a similar pronunciation. Therefore one has, for example, *Annius* for *Hananià, Aster* for *Ester, Faustina* for *Jefè Mazal* or *Mazal Tov,* etc. (25). And so the Jewish name

(25) Levi, *op. cit.,* p.148, n. 74.

31

Haym, meaning *vita,* according to the place of captivity was changed to the Greek *Zosimus* and the Latin *Vitalis* (26). If then the problem of the imprint of the shape of a cross, found in a humble room of this house and constituting more or less the proof of Christians at Herculaneum, cannot be said to be resolved, one can with a large margin of probability maintain that the freedwoman *Vitalis* was of Jewish origin and belonged to that group which had embraced the new faith whose symbol she adored in her modest room (27). One is led to suspect this possibility by the strange proximity of elements as close to the Jewish world as to the Christian.

In the light of such considerations one may try to solve another problem which still presents itself to anyone who looks at the cross of Herculaneum. It obviously was torn by force from the wall in which it left traces in the plaster. But as one scholar (28) has wisely observed, it is difficult to interpret the psychological significance of this act of violence. Could it have been the expression of a religious hatred, or could it also be attributed to the frenzy of the believer himself who, in terror of divine punishment and imminent death, wished to carry away that symbol, attributing to it probably also magical and miracle working power in which he saw his ultimate salvation? Considering the two opposite worlds confronting each other in this house, one is more inclined to the first interpretation than to the second. Two different worlds were in fact separated by a few partitions of wall, but also by opposite conceptions of life. And above everything was a hateful mistress, strong in the right which came from the law, who was capable of denying to a young girl who was born in the

---

(26) Leon, *op. cit.,* p.93.

(27) In regard to an oratory belonging to a family of Jews, it is useful to recall the picture of an oratory, closed by shutters, with the scroll of the law deposited inside, that was found in the Jewish catacomb of Villa Torlonia. It is identical to the one at Herculaneum. See Beer and Lietzman, *Die judische Katacombe der Villa Torlonia in Rom,* Berlin 1930, p.24; A. Maiuri, *La croce di Ercolano,* Rendiconti della Pontificia Accad. Romana di Archeologia Ser.3 col.15 (1939) Roma 1940, pp.216-218.

(28) A. Baldi, *La Pompei cristiano-giudaica,* Cava dei Tirreni 1964, p. 84.

house the right of controlling her own life and her own liberty (29). The mistress, to whom one is indeed inclined to attribute the gesture, was perhaps not sacrilegious but rather expressed revenge for that sign which for some of her servants signified already the redemption from bodily slavery and the promise of liberty to every living creature.

The last discovery, we can relate to the Jewish worlds, was found out at Herculaneum between 1972 and 1973 in a little room of the «Casa dei Cervi». There was discovered a bronze coin of Herod Archelaus (4 b.c.e. - 6 a.c.e.) which on a face has a cluster of grapes with a leaf and Greek inscription HPΩΔOY, wile on the other has a helmet with a caduceus (30).

7 – STABIAE

The most important and most admired monument to be found in the Antiquarium at Stabia is a fine marble sarcophagus on the front face of which are sculptured eleven figures in high relief namely: Apollo and Minerva together with the nine Muses. It is the opinion moreover of some experts that this artistic tableau of Stabia was inspired by a renowned group of statues brought from Ambracio to Rome in the year 178 B.C.E. and placed in the Temple of Hercules Musarum (31). The cover of the sarcophagus has the follow-

---

(29) A. Maiuri, *La Campania al tempo dell'approdo di San Paolo*, Sorrento – Napoli 1991, p.40. Note also that in the trial, the servant *Tamudius*, whose nationality may be Jewish or Arabic, served as a witness to aid *Vitalis*, as will be pointed later, *infra* 39. See G. Pugliese Carratelli, *Tabulae Herculanenses*, Parola del Passato vol. 3, 1948, Fasc.8, pp.165-184 and *Il processo di Giusta*, Prolegomeni vol. 1, 1952, pp.117-119.

(30) V. Tran Tam Tinh, *À la recherche d'Herculanum preromaine*, in: Cronache Pompeiane vol.3, 1977, pp.40-56.

(31) See: F. Di Capua, *Le antichità stabiane conservate nella sala capitolare e le origini del Cristianesimo a Stabia*, Caserta (Tip. F. Russo) ca. 1922-24; N. Terzaghi, *Le Muse in un sarcofago di Castellammare di Stabia*, Mouseion vol. 1, 1923, pp. 245-253; G.B. De Rossi, *Cimitero cristiano di Stabia*, Bollettino di Archeologia Cristiana, Ser.3 vol.4, 1879, pp.118-127; Th. Mommsen, *CIL*, IX, p.84, n.966.

Fig. 8. Cover of sarcophagus with inscription.

ing inscription carved in the middle from which we can observe that it was dedicated to Giulio Longino, an Officer of the Fleet at Miseno, married to a Hebrew named Maria who had commissioned the work for this noble tomb.

Here is the text:

IULIO . LONGINO
PRINCIPALI . COL . MIS.
EX. XR. QUI. VIX. AN. LIII
DIES. LV. IULIA. MARIA. UXOR
B. M. F.

8 – NAPLES

In spite of much evidence for Jewish settlement in the Campanian cities in the first century C. E. we still do not have documents which tell equally of the Jews in Naples. But a place full of ancient Jewish tombs from a later period

34

came to light in November 1908 (32) during the construction of the Caserma di Artiglieria in the Corso Malta, formerly the Corso Orientale, and opposite the principal gate. While excavating the foundation, at a depth of three metres a series of tombs were found with tiles arranged as a roof. The research of Galante assigned the tombstones of this Jewish cemetery to the period of the oldest catacombs of Venosa, that is between the end of the fourth and the middle of the fifth centuries. However, the existence of a cemetery which shows the presence of a well-organized community is the undoubted consequence of an earlier existence, which might reach back to the time of the other Vesuvian cities (33).

Because of this and also because for the first time in these, which are the oldest Neapolitan Jewish inscriptions, one finds the representation of the *Menorah,* or the seven-branched candelabra, it seems fitting to record these inscriptions and comment on them briefly.

It appears that this ancient Neapolitan Jewish cemetery contained numerous tombs and that above some of them were found others, so that they formed two levels of graves, sometimes with two tiles placed on the original base, otherwise on two little walls, in the manner of a sarcophagus. Two tombstones were found here, and there is a broken inscription outside (34).

The first of these tombstones belonged to a certain *Barbarus* son of *Cumanus* coming from Venafrum (Campobasso), as one infers from the epitaph:

(32) G. A. Galante, *Un sepolcreto giudaico recentemente scoperto in Napoli,* in: Memorie della Reale Accademia di Archeologia e Belle Arti di Napoli vol.2, 1913, pp.231-245.

(33) P. A. Bellucci, *Le origini del Cristianesimo e dei cimiteri paleocristiani a Napoli* (Unpublished MS of Father Antonio Bellucci, Librarian of the Biblioteca dei Gerolomini, via Duomo, Naples).

(34) Another Jewish cemetery, but of the thirteenth century, is recorded by Saba Malaspina in his *Rerum sicularum historia.* In speaking of the death of Corradino of Swabia he says that in the Piazza del Mercato, near the early Chiesa del Carmine, a Jewish cemetery was found, but that no traces remained after the building of the Chiesa del Carmine, the Chiesa della Croce and the Piazza del Mercato.

HIC REQUIESCIT IN PACE
BARBARUS FILIUS CUMANI
DE BENAFRI QUI VIXIT AN
NUS PLM XVIII DEPOSI
TUS IDUS IULIAS IND VI

Following the Latin inscription is an acclamation in the Hebrew language which shouts out:

SHALOM AL MENUḤATEḤA
«Peace to your rest».

The second tombstone belonged to a girl, a certain *Herenia* daughter of *Telesinus,* who seems to have been originally from the neighbouring town of Telesia (modern Telese) and had a cognomen analogous to the preceding *Cumanus.* The entire epitaph is:

HIC RE
QUIES
CIT IN PA
CE HERE
NIA FILIA
THELESI
NI ROMEI AN
PLM VIII

Also on this tombstone the *Menorah* can be seen, but the acclamation is lacking. The fragment of the third stone has four letters and halves of two others which make no sense.

Galante, basing his judgment on the criteria of Ascoli and De Rossi, noted that on the basis of the accepted rule for dating Jewish inscription (ancient if in the Greek or Latin language and with an abundance of symbols or medieval if in Hebrew and having a scarcity of symbols), the two stones of our Neapolitan tombs should be attributed to the first category. The formula *Hic requiescit in pace,* and the word *depositus* go back to the end of the fourth century and later,

Fig. 9. The Tombstone of Barbarus

and also the expression *Idus Iulias* which furnishes the consular date makes it possible to date the epitaphs not earlier than fifth century.

But we are led to suspect from the double row of sepulchres, that in this cemetery at Naples even more ancient tombs might be found.

Even if they are not Neapolitans, in fact according to the catalogue by Fiorelli they seem to come from the area of Rome, we judged appropriate to present here two sepulchral stones now at the National Museum, in case they are the object of a deeper interest.

They are even mentioned in Leon's work under the number 460 and 380 but without any photographic document.

The first tombstone (35) tells us about the archon for life (*dia bius*) *Tettius Rufinus Meilitius* who lived 85 years:

TETTIUS RUFINUS
MEILITIUS VICXIT AN
NIS LXXXV
IA BIUS

Fig. 10. Inscription of Tettius Rufinus

(35) Inventory of Naples National Museum n. 4519.
(36) Inventory of Naples National Museum n. 4522.

The second (36) recalls a *Besules* who lived 25 years and is written in Greek characters:

ΛΟΚΟΥ
ΒΕΚΟΥΛΕС
ΑΝΟΥΡΟΡΕ
ΚΕСΗΤΚΕ

Fig. 11.
Inscription
of Besules

that is: sepulchre of Besules, she died at twenty.

CHAPTER III

THE JEWS IN ANCIENT POMPEII

Situated on the shore of a sea which the mouth of the river Sarno made favourable to commerce, the ancient Oscan city of Pompeii must have had since remote times a considerable attraction both for the foreigners who came to settle in fertile Campania, and for the merchants and the sailors from Greece, Phoenicia and the countries of the East, who, in their travels, found the port of Pompeii a happy landing-place.

From the time of the Romanization of Campania the population of the towns grew considerably. Many were the Romans who with the establishment of the colony made their homes at Pompeii, building there luxurious houses and magnificent villas. When relations with countries overseas increased, foreigners coming to sell their wares also prolonged their stay in happy Pompeii until they made a permanent home there. In the retinue of rich and aristocratic Roman families numerous slaves of diverse origin also came. They often succeeded, thanks to their intelligence and ability, in immersing themselves in a notable manner in the economic, social, and even political life of the city. We have, then, a heterogeneous population immortalized by the material gushing out from Vesuvius. Tragic and frightening evidence shows us at times the vigour of life, and at other times the agony of death.

In the midst of this colourful population lived a community of Jews, but we do not know yet its size or details about its development. But some inscriptions, some vague traces here and there, and finally a recently excavated inscription permit that in the history and reconstruction of the life of ancient Pompeii a page may be dedicated to its inhabitants of Jewish origin.

1) Among the Jews at Pompeii was a certain:

YOUDAIKOU

a producer and merchant of wine, both of the choice type, such as Cnidium and of the ordinary *Trughinon*, black as ink. He was of sufficiently comfortable status to have slaves of his own, among whom was the vine-dresser *Felix*. The wine of *Youdaikou* was also consumed in the large *thermopolium* (1) of *L. Vetutius Placidus* (Region I, *insula* viii, entrance 7) on the Via dell'Abbondanza in which were found *amphorae* with the inscription in Greek:

TY FELIX YOUDAIKOU (2).

T Y
ΓΕΛΙΧ
ΙΟΥΔΛΙΚΟΥ

2) The manager of one of the most important hotels of Pompeii, the one installed in the building known as the House of Sallust (VI, ii, 4), was:

A. COSS(ius) LIBAN(us)

whose name definitely reveals freedman status (3). According to Mau (4), with the exception of the south peri-

---

(1) A type of tavern in which warm drinks were served, or kept hot on stoves. See M. Brion, *Pompei ed Ercolano*, Novara 1962, p.126.
(2) *CIL*, IV, 9757. M. Della Corte, *Case ed abitanti in Pompei*, 2. ed., Pompei – Roma 1954, p. 271, J. B. Frey, *Les Juifs à Pompéi*, in: Revue Biblique vol.42, Paris 1953, pp.365-384, see 366.
(3) *CIL*. IV, 4735; Della Corte, *Case ed abitanti in Pompei*, p. 29.
(4) A. Mau, *Pompeii, its Life and Art*, New York – London 1907, p. 287.

style which remained in the possession of the ancient family which owned the entire edifice, all the remaining part had been transformed into one of the better hotels of the city, and *A. Cossius Libanus* was very probably the proprietor or the manager. Was he a Jew? The ethnic name *Libanus*, from the mountain by that name between Palestine and Syria, makes it seem probable (5). The name *Cossius*, the only one to date in Pompeii, confirms the oriental origin of the man. For some the name refers to the *Kossiaioi, Cossiei*, people of *Susiana* (6). But it could also be derived from *Cush*, the country frequently mentioned in the Bible *(Gen.,* 10. 6; *Isaiah*, 18.1; *Ester*, 1.1 passim), which generally refers to Ethiopia or Lower Egypt, with a vague frontier to the south. The Jews had contacts with *Cush*. Such a supposition seems to find an excellent confirmation in another inscription (7) in which we are able to read together the names Cossius and Africanus:

T. Sextius Africanus. Africano Cos(sio)

3) Another:

LIBANOS

was a servant in the Villa of the Mysteries. His name has been found three times where he recorded it in various places in this luxurious edifice (8).

---

(5) This inscription, known only from two eighteenth century Vatican MSS, gives evidence of a Jew who probably came from the city of Arca of Lebanon, home of Alexander Severus. See H.J. Leon, *The Jews of Ancient*, Philadelphia 1960, pp.163-165, 338.

(6) M. Della Corte, *Case ed abitanti in Pompei*, 30. The possession of *tria nomina* reveals the long stay in Pompeii of this freedman of probable Jewish origin.

(7) *CIL*, IV, 5544.

(8) M. Della Corte, *Le iscrizioni della Villa Giuliana o «dei Misteri»*, Memorie della Reale Accademia di Archeologia, Lettere e Belle Arti della Società Reale di Napoli vol.6, 1942, n. 93.

4) M. VALERIUS ABINNERICUS

ΣΥΜΡΝ

ΛΤΕττΛ

ΧΥΙΙΙ   ΙΤΛΥ

Μ ΥΛΙΕΡΙ·αdΙΝΝΕΡΤΟ

was another merchant and wine-producer likewise of freed-man status.

His name, in Hebrew Abner, was found repeated on various wine *amphorae* (9). Some authors however are little inclined to see in the cognomen the Latinised form of Abner; but their arguments are somewhat strange and not absolutely valid (10).

(9) *CIL*, IV, 5630.
(10) For a discussion see Frey, *op. cit.*, 375; A. Mallardo, *La questione dei Cristiani a Pompei*, extract from Rivista di studi pompeiani vol.1, 1934-35, p. 20.

5) Another Jew:

I E S U S

gives information about himself by signing a graffito referring to the world of the amphitheatre. In the inscription he
takes to task the gladiator *Lucius Asicius* by comparing him
to a poor little fish, and not to an invincible champion as the
people wanted (11).

6) Some Jews, considering what was said about *Vitalis* at
Herculaneum, were able to disguise themselves under the
various:

(11) *CIL*, IV, 4287. M. Della Corte, *Revisione di antichi testi*, daily «Roma»,
July 13, 1961, Naples edition.

among whom was the freedman of *Lucius Istacidius*, proprietor of the so-called Villa of the Mysteries. Another *Zosimus*, was manager of a tavern on the Via dell'Abbondanza (III, iv, 1), is famous because he painted on the walls of his shop, for the greater convenience of his customers, the calendar of the markets which were held in the cities of Pompeii, Nola, Nocera, Pozzuoli, Capua and Rome (12).

7) Some names of Jews appear in a very singular inscription, still an object of study, for which up to now a satisfactory explanation has not been found.

It is undoubtedly in the Hebrew language especially the last word which can be read easily as *Lamerhaz*, that is: «for the bath» (13). Here perhaps also appears the name:

IESHUA

This inscription which was discovered in the hall annexed to the so-called House of the Cryptoporticus (I, vi, 2) was already in bad condition when it was recopied by Frey (14) and some of it has now entirely disappeared. This makes attempts at interpretation even more difficult.

(12) *CIL*, IV, 8866. For the cognomen in Rome see H. J. Leon, *The Jews of Ancient*, Philadelphia 1960, p. 104.

(13) *CIL*, IV, 8010; M. Della Corte, *Case ed abitanti in Pompei*, 2. ed., Pompei – Roma 1954, p.280.

(14) The interpretation offered, after the discovery in 1931, by Mosè Ginsburgher is not very convincing. He believes the mutilated names should be read: «Kar... Jesua Shadani (ham) sons of Lenanath have sold to *Vergaz* something that is above the bath»; M. Della Corte, *Fabius Eupor, princeps libertinorum e gli elementi giudaici in Pompei*, Atti dell'Accademia Pontaniana, N. S., vol.3 (1949-50) Napoli 1951, pp.347 ff. believes the sale concerned some property above the Forum Baths.

8) Three graffiti on the wall of a tavern on the Via dei Diadumeni (15) is present a certain:

I O N A S

IONAS CVN FILIITO
HIC
FILLAT

and also furnish information about the baseness of his habits. True or not as the facts might be (so also for a certain *Libanis*, perhaps also a Jew), this reflects above all the easy mockery to which the Jews more than others were exposed (16).

It is possible to understand in this way the word *verpa*, which by Martial (17) and by Juvenal (18) is used in an offensive manner indicating «circumcision». In Pompeii, the term appears only one time referring to a person:

HYSOCRIRE PUER NATALIS VERPA TE SALUTAT
o Hisocrirus, the boy Natalis, *verpa,* greets you.
NATALIS VERPA
O *verpa* Natalis (19)

and another time it is used in an indeterminate form:

ET EGO VERPA QUI LEGO (20)
And I *verpa* who read

This term however was also used in the popular Latin language to refer to a generic injury. Nothing authorizes us to conclude that in the Pompeian examples it was used with specific reference to the Jews.

---

(15) *CIL,* IV, 2402-2404, 2406. A. W. Van Buren, *Epigraphical salvage from Pompeii*, American Journal of Philology, vol. 47, 1926, p. 177.
(16) M. Della Corte, *Case ed abitanti in Pompei*, 2.ed., Pompei – Roma 1954, p. 29, note.
(17) Martial, 14. 104.
(18) Juvenal, 7. 82. 6.
(19) *CIL,* IV, 1655, 1375.
(20) *CIL,* IV, 2360.

9) Another enigma up to this time, but now well identified by virtue of the recent epigraphical discovery, is the singular figure of the freedman:

FABIUS EUPOR

a rich wine merchant, politician, and financier (21) whose home was on the Via Consolare, immediately to the south of the former Excavation office. An electoral notice:

CVSPIVM PANSAM AED (ilem) FABIVS
EVPOR PRINCEPS LIBERTINORVM ROGAT (22)

which represents him as chief of the *libertini* suggests two interpretations as to his identity.

From historical evidence we know that the Jews from Rome and the other compatriots from Alexandria and from Cyrene maintained their own synagogue in Jerusalem, called «The Synagogue of the Freedmen» because the greater part of the members belonged to the freedmen class (23). For some then *Eupor* was a kind of *archisynagogus* of the Jewish community at Pompeii and as recognized head of this community he asked his coreligionists to support the candidature of Cuspius Pansa (24).

For others, who recalled the evidence in Cicero, this Fabius Eupor would have been instead the *patronus* of a rather large corporation made up of the freed slaves and freedmen, which like all other organizations took part in the electoral contests. It

---

(21) *CIL*, IV, 120.
(22) *CIL*, IV, 117.
(23) Acts, 6. 9; Leon, *op. cit.*, 19.
(24) This interpretation is supported by G. B. De Rossi, *Bullettino di archeologia cristiana*, Serie 1, Anno 2, No. 9, Sept. 1864, pp. 69-70 and No. 12, Dec. 1864, pp. 92-93, 95; M. Della Corte, *Fabius Eupor, princeps libertinorum e gli elementi giudaici in Pompei*, Atti dell'Accademia Pontaniana, N. S., vol.3 (1949-50) Napoli 1951, pp.347-353. The name *Eupor* is also found in the Jewish catacombs in Rome where it belongs to a Jew buried with his son *Sabbatius*. See Leon, *op. cit.*, 313. For the passages in the Jewish Philo and in Tacitus, in regard to this interpretation (with confirmation of the story referred to by the latter, in Josephus and in Suetonius) see *CIL*, IV, 117, commentary, Frey *op. cit.*, 370.
(25) For the supporters of this interpretation see Th. Mommsen, *Rheinisckes Museum*, 19, 1864, p. 156; Zangemeister in *CIL*, IV, 117. See also Frey, *op. cit.*, 371.

is true that in the official language the head of an organization was not designated by the title *princeps*. But we should not be surprised at this usage if we consider the popular language of Pompeii, especially in the acclamation in which, for example, the citizen Maius receives the title of *princeps coloniae,* and a woman, Cestilia, that of *regina pompeianorum* (25).

The candidate Pansa seems to have been exceedingly prompt in securing for himself the recommendations of the religious circles. In obtaining aid from the Jews he was also supported in his rise to the aedileship by the followers of Isis, as is apparent from the notice:

> CVSPIVM PANSAM AED (ilem)
> POPIDIVS NATALIS CLIENS CVM
> ISIACIS ROG (at)

also by the priest Amandus:

> PANSAM AED (ilem)
> AMANDVS SACERDOS ROG (at) (26).

10) On the so-called Via della Fortuna (VI. xiii. 6) was the home of M. Terentius Eudoxus. The peristyle of this house had been transformed into a textile shop in which humble labourers worked. On the wall of the portico, graffiti record their names, with details about their work, along with other words and obscene phrases. We learn that among the employees was:

> MARIA

and there was recorded also the amount of work she had finished *(pensi stamen)* (27).

---

(26) *CIL,* IV, 1011, 7900. For Fabius Eupor as chief man of the community of Jews at Pompei, see also G. Onorato, *Iscrizioni pompeiane. La vita pubblica,* Florence 1957, pp.165-166.

(27) *CIL,* IV, 1507. For the theory that the name Maria is the feminine of Marius, and the refutation see A. Mau, *Pompeii. Its Life and Art,* New York – London 1899, p. 18.

(28) This is the view of M. Della Corte, *Case ed abitanti in Pompei,* 2. ed., Pompei – Roma 1954, p. 98.

Fig. 12. Pompeii, Via Consolare

Photo Alinari

51

Mention is also made in the same shop of the weaver *Vesbius Tamudianus* who because of his ethnic name *Tamudianus*, however, has been said to be from the city of *Tamud*, and therefore a Jew (28). It should be observed however that the city referred to in antiquity by that name, together with the people of the *Tamudieni*, was part of Arabia Felix and that never, even in the period of greatest expansion, was the State of Israel joined to that region (29). Therefore the freedman Vesbius Tamudianus was certainly not of Jewish, but of Arabic nationality.

11) Of servile condition however, was:

MARTHA

a slave in the House of A. Rustius Verus also known as the House of the Centenary, (IX. viii, 6) made the butt of a jest written on the wall of the latrine of the house (30).

12) Still another slave:

MARIA

(29) *Enciclopedia Italiana Treccani, s. v. «Tamudieni»*.
(30) *CIL*, IV, 3763, 5244. The name *Martha* probably derives from the aramaic *Maràh*, meaning «Lady». In the catacombs at Rome the name Martha appears only once, that of Maria eight times. See Leon, *op cit.*, 105.

Fig. 13. Pompeii, The thermopolium of the *Asellinae*

served together with the Greek *Aegle*, and with the Asian *Smyrna* in the tkermopolium of *Asellinae* on the Via dell'Abbondanza (IX ii. 2). She was also interested in the electoral propaganda, and recommended the candidature of Cnaeus Helvius Sabinus (31) He, however, little welcomed such support on the part of girls of such humble social class and had a spy to hide the recommendation under a large cover of white plaster (32)

13) Perhaps another Jew was:

LIBANIS

LIBANIS
)'ELAT
A Γ

(31) *CIL*, IV, 7866. M. Della Corte, *Notizie degli Scavi,* 1911, p. 455; M. D'Avino, *La donna a Pompei*, Napoli 1964, pp. 29-49.
(32) M. Della Corte, *Notizie degli Scavi,* 1911, pp.455-456.

a man of not very edifying habits if we believe denunciations found in an inscription (33).

14) And finally a servant:

MARIA

is mentioned in the so-called House of the Fourth Style (I. viii, 17) where, at the right of the rear door, on the bare plaster one reads: *Maria es* (34).

At this point some remarks regarding the Jewish names in ancient Pompeii should be made. The inventory of names listed in this chapter is without doubt incomplete. Nor can it be denied that some persons of Semitic name believed to be Jewish might not be Jews at all. But even if the evidence makes identification sometimes all too vague and uncertain, it is necessary to pause to consider an important fact. No Jewish name is found in the oldest inscriptions; both the electoral notices written on the walls and the graffiti with Jewish names are from the last years of the city and therefore shortly before the year 79 C. E. Now in this period there was no migration of Semitic people into Campania except the great flood of Jewish slaves that came into Italy after the taking of Jerusalem in 70 C. E. Since the increase of Semitic names in the population of Pompeii is seen to accompany the arrival of the surviving Israelites, the first ought for the most part to be attributed to the second.

Even if the inventory of Jewish names reveals little, it makes possible an interesting analysis. Of the fourteen names recorded, seven are Semitic. This is significant if one bears in mind that in the Jewish inscriptions from the catacombs in Rome scarcely 13% have Semitic names. It is, on the other hand evident that the phenomenon of adjusting to the surroundings can also be verified for the Jews at Pompeii.

(33) *CIL*, IV, 2028. It is evident that the intention here is to mock at that wretched slave, accused to prostitute herself dirt-cheap (3 *asses*).
(34) *CIL*, IV, 8224; M. Della Corte, *Notizie degli Scavi*, 1946, p.123, n.355.

Among the new customs there was that of adopting the names in use in the new country. There are also some examples of composite names, and in this case the Latin one precedes the Greek or the Semitic one. These names indicate that the process of the Latinization of the Jewish community at Pompeii had already begun, even if it had not become complete.

CHAPTER IV

JEWISH REPRESENTATIONS
AND EVIDENCE IN POMPEIAN ART

WALL PAINTINGS

More than two centuries of almost uninterrupted excavation gives to Pompeii the incontestable pre-eminence for the richest documentation of wall paintings and of mosaic pavements for the period which dates from the end of the second century B. C. E to 79 C. E. If today the National Museum at Naples is the best place for seeing the objects represented in Pompeian pictures, nevertheless only Pompeii, with its fascinating setting, succeeds in giving a complete idea of a city in which pictorial decoration had reached a universal use. It is found not only in the houses of every social class, but even in the workshops and places of business which appear everywhere throughout the city.

A careful observation allows one to group the motifs of Pompeian painters into two categories. The first has classical tendencies in which the forms are perfect, but cold and submissive to Hellenistic and neo-classic models. The second, on the other hand, reacts to old outlines with an infinite variety of themes which illustrate now personages and episodes of classical mythology, and at other times, aspects of nature and of family life, the latter rendered often with a portrayal and a flavor sometimes very near to the modern by virtue of an impressionistic handling due to Alexandrian influence. In this type of picture is found also a refined sense of caricature to which belong the scenes of the pigmies and to which ought to be assigned the two pictures which recall Biblical themes.

1. THE JVDGMENT OF SOLOMON

In 1882, in excavating house VIII, v, 24, great was the interest aroused by the discovery of a series of pictures

Fig. 14. Wall Painting with «The Judgment of Solomon». Naples, National Museum, Inv. n. 113197

which adorned the garden (1). The first two represented the valley of the Nile, animated by pigmies, crocodiles, hippopotamuses, and ibis. The third and fourth showed typical wild beasts of the African fauna. The fifth pictured a marsh with every kind of aquatic plant and an ibis seizing a toad. But it is in the last scene, a long one, and the most interesting because of its originality, that the Biblical world finds a diverting caricature in the parody of the celebrated judgment of Solomon (2). The action unfolds in a praetorium where it is acted out with marionett-like gesture by dwarfish and deformed actors, in the guise of pigmies with very large heads and bodies and ridiculously slender arms and legs.

The characters in the picture are divided into two groups. In the first a group of judges is seated on a kind of platform. Among the judges is King Solomon with a sceptre in his right hand. In front of the court, at the bottom of the

(1) A. Sogliano, *Notizie degli Scavi*, 1882, pp. 323-324.
(2) The painting can be seen in the National Museum at Naples, Inv. n. 113197.

picture, are some soldiers with helmets and shining armours. In the centre on the chopping block is placed the body of the innocent young boy ready to be cut in two by a large knife gripped by the executioner. In the second group are pictured, in a very expressive manner, the two mothers, the true one almost reduced to a heap or rags. Some spectators can be glimpsed curious and at the same time frightened by what was about to take place before their eyes (3).

The analogy of the Pompeian painting to the Biblical account (*I Kings* 3, 16 ff.) is too evident to leave any doubt about the content of the painting doubtful. It is only necessary to clarify the conditions under which this kind of painting was developed. It is certainly of a foreign style, probably (Alexandrian. In the first century of the Empire commercial relations between our peninsula and Egypt were active, and the principal harbours for trade with Alexandria, the emporium of Pharaonic lands, were Campanian Pozzuoli and Pompeii. But it is a fact universally recognized that together with their goods, the Egyptians also transmitted to the city of Pompeii their artistic motifs Pompeian art borrowed from the Alexandrian especially the pleasant and spirited scenes of the life of pigmies, and the great hunts along the Nile river. Now it is also recorded that in Alexandria the hostility toward the Jews was particularly violent, and manifested itself not only with agitation in the public square, but also by ridiculing the Jewish customs and traditions, which the first Greek version of the Bible, known as the Septuagint, had divulged and made known (4).

It is possible then to conclude that the city of origin of the Pompeian painting of the Judgment of Solomon was

(3) For description see A. Maiuri, *Le peinture romaine*, Génève 1953, p. 114. For the bibliography of the picture, consult G. B. Frey, *Les Juifs à Pompéi* in Revue biblique, vol.42, Paris 1953, p. 375; O. Elia, *Pitture murali e mosaici nel Museo Nazionale di Napoli*, Roma 1932, p. 59; A. Baldi, *La Pompei cristiano-giudaica*, Cava dei Tirreni 1964, p. 19.

(4) A. Bludau, *Juden und Judenverfolungen in alten Alexandria*, Munich 1906, p. 1 ff.

Alexandria, and that the Pompeian artist had copied an Alexandrian model, as he had done for the other pictures with which he had decorated the garden. However, since the people in the painting were clothed in Roman dress, and the Biblical scene was treated as a caricature, it has seemed to many more than evident that the unknown master of the house desired to have in view in his own garden a pictorial motif which satirized the Jews of Pompeii, and also declared his aversion towards that people (5).

2. The Story of Jonah

In this same series of pictures there is another which also has the river Nile as scenic background. Here a pigmy standing on the back of a large hippopotamus is striking the animal with a rounded object. A second pigmy is attempting to pull out of the enormous throat of the pachyderm a third compan-

Fig. 15. Scene with pigmies. Naples National Museum, Inv. n. 113196.

(5) D. Mallardo, *La questione dei Cristiani a Pompei*, Rivista Studi Pompeiani 1, Napoli 1935, pp.116-165, 217-261. For the other interpretation see Alexander Moret, *De Bocchori rege*, Paris 1903, pp.58-61, fig.6 and Frey, *op. cit.*, 381-382.

Fig. 16. Naples, National Museum, Inv. n. 113195

ion who has evidently been swallowed by the monster. In the distance, on the river, can be seen a ship loaded with wine (6).

But what is the significance of this picture? One widely held interpretation maintains that this painting as well as the preceding one is nothing more than a Nile scene with pigmies, which was a favourite with Alexandrian painters. But there are some who maintain that it is possible to discern also in this painting a Biblical theme: the parable of the story of Jonah, here transformed into a pigmy and swallowed not by a whale, but by an monstrous hippopotamus (7). This interpretation becomes plausible if one attributes to the unknown commissioner of the painting the same attitude toward the Jews which is glimpsed in the parody of the Judgment of Solomon*.

(6) A. Sogliano, *Notizie degli Scavi*, 1882, pp. 322-323. The painting can be seen in the National Museum at Naples, Inv. n. 113196. See very similar the painting found in the same house: A. Soglianoi *Notizie degli Scavi*, 1882, p. 322, now in the National Museum at Naples, Inv. n. 113195.

(7) Frey, *op. cit.*, p. 368; P. Gusman, *Pompéi*, Paris 1899, p. 419; H. Leclerq, *Manuel d'archéologie chrétienne*, Paris 1907, vol. 2, p. 651, fig. 407.

(*) Cfr. from the same house the similar and companion painting now in Naples, National Museum, Inv. n. 113195.

JEWISH ELEMENTS IN SCULPTURE

With regard to sculpture Pompeii is a centre of originality. The works brought to light, whether imported, or created by sculptors locally, represent many diverse influences. Pompeian sculpture is thus from period to period Italic, Hellenistic, and finally Roman art.

There is no space here to discuss the works of local production, even though such art acquired great importance in Pompeii. Imported works permitted the admiration of perfect copies of Greek masterpieces, while those of local manufacture revealed the Hellenistic-Roman taste and the culture of the inhabitants of the city (8). But there also remain vivid reminders of the innumerable statuettes that were Hellenistic originals or imitations of Hellenistic originals.

3. THE PLACENTARIUS. THE PASTRY-COOK STATUETTES

In the House of the rich merchant Publius Cornelius Tages (I. vii. 10), who had business contact with Egypt and Alexandria, there were found among the other household goods in bronze and in terra cotta, four statuettes made of gilded bronze of pastry-cooks holding magnificent silver trays (9). Each of the four sculptures represents in a rather vulgar manner, by laying excessive stress on each part of the very thin body, an old peddler, completely naked, in the act of uttering his cry of sale, his left hand placed on his throat and carrying on his right hand the plate with the hot cakes of milk and honey.

It should be mentioned here that a similar picture of life,

---

(8) One sees for example the extraordinary gigantic head of Jove, of the Otricoli type, (now in the National Museum at Naples) which dominated the *Capitolium*, or the bronze statues of Apollo and Diana, Campanian reproductions of Greek works in the east *porticus* of the Temple of Apollo at Pompeii.

(9) The House of Tagetes is known also as the House of the Ephebe, because in it was found the statue of an Ephebe, adapted for use as a lamp-stand near the dining table in the garden. See A. Maiuri, *Notizie degli Scavi*, 1927, 32-33.

Fig. 17. The placentarius, Naples, National Museum

Fig. 18. The placentarius, particular

that of the sausage peddler, is found in the verse of the salacious poet of imperial Rome:

> *Fumantia qui tomacla raucus*
> *Circumfert tepidis cocus popinis*
> (Mart. *Ep.* 1. 42. 9.)

Now if one considers the strong singularity of the features of the pastry-cook's face, the extraordinarily elongated skull, the unkempt condition of the beard and hair, the nose, short and sharp-pointed at the tip, it is impossible not to agree that the physical traits moulded by the artist are unquestionably those of an Oriental, and more precisely, according to the competent judgment of one scholar (10), of an Alexandrian Jew.

In Alexandria, when it was seen that the Jews loved to withdraw themselves and above all that they abhorred the cult of the gods, the most incredible stories and false accusations began to circulate against them. The isolation of the Jews in Alexandria, understandable under certain aspects was repaid with humiliating conditions of work, contempt, disgusting insults and obscene jests (11). It seems then that in the grotesque and mocking representations of the peddlers of cakes the unknown Alexandrian artist intended to represent more or less in a veiled manner (12) a Jewish vendor, making him however the object of derision.

---

(10) A. Maiuri, *La raffigurazione del Placentarius*, Bollettino d'Arte, 19, 1925-26, pp.268-275.

(11) G. Ricciotti, *Storia d'Israele*, Torino 1960. vol. 2, p. 231.

(12) Of another opinion is A. Della Seta, *Il Nudo nell'Arte*, Milano 1936 who points out that the fact that the *Placentarius is* not circumcised makes it impossible for him to be a Jew. But he identifies the cake-vendor as an oriental. It should be pointed out however that in Jerusalem by the time of Antiochus IV, Epiphanes, about 170 B.C.E. this practice was not always followed. When gymnasiums were erected in the Greek manner, where youths exercised nude, circumcision made Jewish youths the object of mockery and of derision on the part of non-Jews (Gentiles), so that numerous parents no longer circumcised their sons. See *I Maccabees* 1. 17; Ricciotti, *op. cit.*, pp. 235, 262.

Fig. 19. Hotel of the Jews. Pompeii, VII, xi, 11, 14.

Fig. 20. Hotel of the Jews. Reconstruction

4. The Statuette on the Cooking Utensil

In the Vicolo del Lupanare, occupying all the northwest corner of *insula* XI of *regio* VII, is the most noteworthy hotel of the city, a large building with two storeys and a capacity of 25 beds. It had a large garden adorned with cool and gracious pergolas which offered to the customers the comfort of cheerful meals in the open. On the outside of this edifice there was among the other dependencies also a *caupona* or tavern, in which the customers were offered the famous *lympha Romanensis*. As in the past century, so also in the present, this building which is commonly known as the «Hotel of the Christians», and in some modern guides as the «Hotel of the Jews», continues to be the object of study though for a variety of reasons (13).

Nevertheless it can be definitely stated that in this public place there was found unequivocal evidence of primitive Christianity together with other evidence for the presence of Jews. What was seen at Herculaneum is also true at Pompeii; the new faith sank its first roots into the bosom of a Jewish circle now oriented toward the *impulsore Chresto*.

And it was also in this hotel that other evidence was discovered which referred to the Jewish circle in Pompeii. On a characteristic bronze cooking utensil or *foculus authepsa*, shaped as the knob of the lid, was a statuette of an emaciated prisoner, a barbarian, almost entirely nude save for a loincloth around the hips; his hands are bound behind his back by means of a heavy chain which served the practical purpose of securing the lid to the container (14). The thick unkempt beard, the head with long hair, the upturned face, leave no doubts; one is dealing with a Jewish prisoner, in the same guise of a chained barbarian that can be seen pictured on the bronze money coined by Gaius Sosius, governor of

(13) M. Della Corte, *L'albergo dei Cristiani*, Civiltà, vol. 3, 1942, n. 9, pp. 73-80; W. F. Jashemski, *A pompeian copa*, The Classical Journal, vol. 59, n.8, May 1964, pp. 344 ff.
(14) Now in the National Museum at Naples, Inv. n. 73879.

Fig. 21. The *foculus authepsa*, Naples, National Museum, Inv. n. 73879.

Fig. 22. The *foculus authepsa*, Cover

Syria, to commemorate the first capture of Jerusalem in 37 B.C.E. (15). The expression of the countenance rendered in a gesture of open defiance and rebellion, strengthens the supposition that the artist had wished to represent in this attitude the «unrestrainable» spirit of the irredentist Jews living and working in Judaea, and in all the Jewish Diaspora of the same period in which the Sanctuary of Jerusalem was destroyed and the Jewish people began their sad exile.

Fig. 23. Bronze money of Gaius Sosius

5. THE JEW OF THE SHIEL

A few years ago the difficult work of clearing away the area outside the south wall of the ancient city was accomplished. At the beginning of July 1953 there came to light

(15) Josephus, *A.J.* 14. 176; H. A. Grueber, *British Museum Catalogue, Rome Rep.*, vol. 2, p. 509.

Fig. 24. Pompeii, Tomb of a warrior

between the Porta Nocera and the Amphitheatre well over twenty mausoleums set in rows along the road and important not only for their architecture, but also for their inscriptions. One of these tombs, catalogued as number 13, offers the most recent likeness of a Jew. It has features similar to those of the statuette on the kettle lid even though it differs in its overall form.

The absence of the tombstone does not permit us to know the name and the social condition of the owner of the sepulchre, but motifs decorating the front of the monument permit us to reconstruct the personality of the deceased, who certainly must have been a warrior. In fact on the white walls of the tomb in bas-relief are depicted the characteristic arms of the Roman soldier: a long lance with the tip turned up, a sturdy sword suspended from a belt of leather, a short dagger hanging from a chain belt, and right in the middle the characteristic *parmula,* the round shield edged with wide red bands.

In the centre of the shield, strongly sculptured by the

70

Fig. 25. The *parmula*, bust of barbarian

delicate work of the chisel, stands out the small bust of a barbarian, with short beard on the chin, a head of tufted hair, and a cloak tied on his breast. The countenance is manifestly sad, and the head bent down toward the ground expresses a tragic anguish. But of such people is the conquered, confined as a symbol of ignominy on the shield of a conqueror who truly seems to have supported the Vergilian precept: *parcere subiectis et debellare superbos*. In what war did the unknown owner of this tomb fight?

By its construction and decoration this tomb can defi-

71

nitely be assigned to the last building period at Pompeii, the years immediately preceding 79 C. E. During this time the only military events worthy of notice were those connected with the Jewish war of 70 and the destruction of Jerusalem, in which the unknown Pompeian must surely have taken part. This belief is strengthened by an attribute clearly visible behind the head of the captive, an attribute which reminds one of the type of Flavian coinage with the legend *IVDEA CAPTA*. Vespasian, having deposited in the Temple of Peace the treasures taken from Jerusalem, issued commemorative money which showed on the reverse a palm, the symbol of Judaea, between the figures of a mourning woman and a man bound in chains (16), Branches of palm and bunches of dates stand out behind the bust of the small figure on the tomb. This settles all doubts regarding the nationality of the prisoner and permits us to consider the sculpture another artistic document at Pompeii pertaining to the Jewish people (17).

6. THE AMPHORAS OF GARUM

Several inscriptions found on clay amphoras have been reconstructed as follows:

MUR(ia) CAST(a) or CAST(imonialia)
GAR(um) CAST(um) or CAST(imoniale) (18)

in which some scholars see a reference to the Jews at Pompeii (19). They justify this interpretation by a passage in Pliny (*N. H.*, 31, 95): *Aliud vero (garum) castimoniarum superstitioni etiam sacrisque Iudeaeis dicatum, quod fit e piscibus squama carentibus*, in which he indicates by this name a special sauce

(16) H. J. Leon, *The Jews of Ancient Rome*, Philadelphia 1960, p. 29; H. Mattingly and E. A. Sydenham, *The Roman Imperial Coinage*, vol. 2, 63, 73, 127.
(17) For the tomb see A. Maiuri, *Pompei. Sterro dei cumuli e isolamento della cinta murale*, Bollettino d'arte, Ser. 4 vol. 45, January-June 1960, pp. 166-179.
(18) *CIL*, IV, 2569, 2609, 2611, 5660, 5661, 5662.
(19) A. Mau, *Pompeji in Leben und Kunst*, Leipzig 1900, p. 17; E. Schurer, *Geschichte des judischen Volkes im Zeitalter J. C.*, Leipzig 1909, vol. 3, p. 67, n. 113.

(garum) made from pickled fish without scales and used by the Jews in their fasting or abstinence. But Pliny is in great error, for the Mosaic Law definitely prohibits the eating of fish without scales (*Leviticus* 11. 9; *Deut.* 14 10). Moreover, in Jewish abstinence absolute fasting was observed.

If one wishes to see a reference to the Jews in the conjectured reconstruction of these amphora inscriptions one should read: *MUR(ia) CAST(a)* and *GAR(um) CAST(um)* and not *CAST(imo*nale). For, as has been said, neither *garum castimoniale,* nor any kind of food could be used in time of abstinence.

But there is another great difficulty for those who believe that they can see in the inscriptions an allusion to a sauce for the Israelites. There is no indication on the amphoras of the kind of fish from which the *garum* was made. How could the Jews have known if it was lawful for them to eat it? We know however that fasting or abstinence as practised in various *mystery cults.* Tertullian (20) and numerous other writers attest that the followers of Isis, Apis, and Cybele prepared themselves for the celebration of some of their solemnities by abstaining from some foods, while Palladius calls *liquamen castimoniale* a variety of condiment permitted to the members of the cults observing abstinence (21). So it can be concluded that the inscriptions on these amphoras very likely indicated that these vases contained *garum,* but that it was intended only for the followers of those cults, and not for the Jews. Lacking specific identification, the Jews observing the Mosaic Law would not have been able to use the sauce, because there were no guarantees that the product had been manufactured in conformity with their religious laws (22).

---

(20) *De Jejunis* 2.; Apuleius, initiated into the mysteries of Isis, practised *inaninam castimoniam* which consisted in abstaining from food coming from animals. See Apuleius, *Metamorphoses,* 2. 19, 28, 30; Jerome (*Epist.* 107. 10) speaks of abstinence from particular foods on the part of the followers of Isis and of Cybele, on the occasion of certain solemnities: *Faciant hoc cultores Isidis et Cibelis qui gulosa abstinentia phasides aves et turtures vorant.*

(21) *Opus agricolturae* 3. 25: *liquamen de piris castimoniale sic fiet.*

(22) For the argument see D. Mallardo, *La questione dei Cristiani a Pompei,* 1935, Extr. p.14.

CHAPTER V

BIBLICAL VOICES IN POMPEII

In a city such as Pompeii, in which a good part of the events and gossip of the town was faithfully recorded on the plaster of the walls, the only written testimony which refers to the destruction of the city does not come from a pagan voice, but curiously echoes motifs of Biblical derivation. It recalls scenes of mourning and of terror which had overtaken, in the same measure as the Vesuvian population, other peoples and fertile districts of Palestine.

The probable work of a Jew, perhaps also a convert to the new religion, was the inscription written on the wall of a humble house (IX, i, 26) with clear reference to the book of Genesis (13.13: 19. 24):

1. SODOM(A) GOMOR(RA) (1)

It was traced with charcoal in large black letters during the catastrophe as a terrible sentence of condemnation. To a Jew, because of the resemblance of its destruction to that of

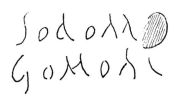

(1) *CIL*, IV, 4976, now in the National Museum at Naples, Inv. n. 114323. E. LE BLANT, Comptes-rendus de l'Acad. des Inscript. Ser.4 vol.12 (1884) Paris 1885, pp.143-147; A. MAU, Bull. dell'Instituto di Corrisp. Archeol. 1885, pp.97-98; E. NESTLE, *Ein Spur des Christentums in Pompeji?*, Zeitschrift neutest. Wissenschaft 5, 1904, pp.167-168; M. GUARDUCCI, Rendic.Accad. dei Lincei, Classe scienze morali Ser.8 vol.15, 1960, pp.5-6.

the two cursed cities, the divine punishment of Pompeii appeared evident in the rain of fire.

2. THE MAGIC SQUARE

The enigmatic inscription, the so-called «Magic Square» (*), for a long time has occupied and still occupies scholars of archaeology and philosophy. Its discovery has been verified twice at Pompeii: the first time back in 1925, in a graffi-

Fig. 26. Inscription of ROTAS-SATOR

* The inscription of the Magic-Squarer, together with that of the Cherem, has been placed in the Antiquarium at Pompeii.

to, unfortunately mutilated, in the house of Paquius Proculus, the second time in 1936, complete, on one of the numerous columns in the west portico of the Grand Palaestra. It was written as follow (2):

```
R O T A S
O P E R A
T E N E T
A R E P O
S A T O R
```

The formula must have been widely spread throughout the vast area of the Roman Empire and also carried by the garrison legions. In 1937 during the excavations at Dura Europos in Mesopotamia it appeared five times all from a period before 256 C.E. for it was only in that year that the Roman troops stationed there abandoned the city (3). Once it was found in remote Britain during excavations at Cirencester in the county of Gloucester (4). It was also found in Egypt, where in the fourth or fifth century it assumed the form of an amulet written on papyri or on parchment (5). In Capadocia it was found in cave paintings that can be dated between the ninth and eleventh centuries (6).

By the beginning of the sixteenth century the formula was used with obvious magical significance and was then spread everywhere with the development of the occult sci-

(2) For a more detailed treatment of this subject see the scholarly work of A. Baldi, *La Pompei cristiano-giudaica*, Cava dei Tirreni 1964, already cited, from which we have drawn in part. For the formula of the magic square see M. Della Corte, *Notizie degli Scavi*, 1929, p. 449; Id., *Il Crittogramma del «Pater Noster» rinvenuto a Pompei*, Rendiconti della Pontificia Accademia Romana di Archeologia, Ser.3 vol.12 (1936) Roma 1937, pp.397-400.

(3) M. Rostovtezeff, *Annali della Reale Scuola Normale di Pisa*, 3, 1934, 103 ff.; *The Excavations at Dura Europos*, V Prelim. Report, 1934, p. 159.

(4) *American (The) Journal of Archaeology*, 56, 1899, p. 320.

(5) See *Dictionnaire d'Archéologie Chrétienne et de Liturgie*, and *Encyclopaedia of Religion and Ethics*, 3, Edinburgh 1908-21, pp. 392-472, s. v. «Charms and Amulets».

(6) G. de Jerphanion, *La formule magique SATOR AREPO*, in: Recherches de Science Religieuse, 25, Paris 1935, pp. 188-225.

ences, by the works of Cornelius Agrippa, Paracelsus von Hohenheim and Athanasius Kircher. But by this time it was used with an inversion in the order of the words which were arranged in the following order:

S A T O R
A R E P O
T E N E T
O P E R A
R O T A S

In was last discovered in 1951 in the Low Pyrenees at Arudy, incised on a container made of horn, together with other cabalistic notations and with the date in which it was made, 1871 (7). About the same time it appeared in Ethiopia in this very curious form:

SADOR, ALADOR, DAMET, ADERA, RODAS (8)

The opinions of scholars are divided in regard to this formula, which with the passage of the years assumed a pro-phylactic character so that it was used in exorcism and other magic practices (9). Some believe it is an early document of Christianity. Others believe that nothing of that kind can be seen in it.

It was taken as a Christian formula in the interesting in-terpretation in which the two scholars Grosser (10) and

(7) The interpretazion of the enigmatic formula offered by Gaston Letonnelier *(Congrès des Sociétés des Savantes in Grenoble)* on 17 April, 1952, is not very convincing. He suggest the words should be read: «Sat orAre poTen(tia) et Opera (a) Rota s(ervant)». For the refutation see M. Della Corte, *Case ed abi-tanti in Pompei*, pp. 394-395.

(8) D. Atkinson, *The Origin and Date of the «SATOR» Word-square*, Journal (The) of Ecclesiastical History, 2, London 1951, p. 14.

(9) J. Carcopino, *Le Christianisme du «carré magique»*, in: Museum Helveticum 5, 1948, p. 22. He believes the *Magic square* is of Celtic origin, be-cause of the word *Arepo,* and that it was traced in Pompeii after the catastrophe. For the rejection of Carcopinòs theory see A. Maiuri, *Sulla datazione del «Quadrato Magico» o Criptogramma cristiano a Pompei.* Rendiconti dell'Accad. di Archeol. Lettere e BB.AA. di Napoli, N.S. 28 (1953), Napoli 1954, pp.101 ff.

(10) F. Grosser, *Ein neuer Vorschlag zur Deutung der Sator-Forrnel,* Archiv für Religionswissenschaft, 24, Freiburg 1926, pp. 165-169.

Agrell (11) collaborated in 1925. They noted that the twenty-five letters of the five words properly arranged represent a cross in which each arm forms the expression *Pater Noster,* with two additional pairs of A-O corresponding to the two letters which St. John in the Apocalypse defines the divinity: *Ego sum alfa et omega, principium et finis.* Of course in Latin territory the omega was transcribed with the O. In regard to this Ausonius said that the *omega* and the o *graecum compensant romulea vox O.*

```
                 P
                 A
    A            T            O
                 E
                 R
      P A T E R N O S T E R
                 O
                 S
    A            T            O
                 E
                 R
```

The documentation of the prayer of the *Pater Noster* was an important discovery for it was regarded as proof of the presence of Christians in Pompeii. The *Pater Noster* was believed to have been recited in the last years of the first century but only in the eastern regions of the Empire. The discovery of the use of Latin in the western liturgy was also important, for it was commonly believed that up to the third century only Greek served as the liturgical language in the West.

De Jerphanion (12) is the chief spokesman for the opposite opinion. Rejecting the position of Grosser and of Agrell

(11) S. Agrell, *Runornas talmystik och dess antika förebild,* (Skrifter utgivna av Vetenskaps-Societen I Lund, 6) Lund 1927, pp. 31 ff.

(12) G. de Jerphanion, *Une nouvelle hypotèse sur l'origine du carré magique: Rotas Opera,* in: La Voix des Monuments. Études d'archéologie, Nouvelle Série, Paris-Rome 1938, pp. 90-94.

Fig. 27. Drawing of the
SATOR-ROTAS

(13), he accepted that of Cumont (14), maintaining that the words of the magic square were extracted from a passage in the Bible, namely the vision of Ezekiel in the following passage.

«I looked: and behold a stormy wind came from the north, and a great cloud and fire flashing forth with brightness all about it, and in the centre a kind of lightning within a great fire. And in the middle of this there was the likeness of four creatures. And they had the appearance of men, but each one had four faces and one four wings...

«And as I looked at the living creatures. there appeared upon the earth beside the creatures a wheel Oil each of their four sides. The appearance of the wheels and their construction was like the stone of Tarsus and the four had the same likeness, and their construction was that of a wheel within another wheel. *Moving, they went on four sides and they were not turning as they went.* (Ezekiel 1. 4-6, 15-17).

«And the Lord said to him, «Go into the middle of the city, through Jerusalem, and mark with a *tau* the foreheads of the men who groan and grieve

(13) G. de Jerphanion, *A propos des nouveaux exemplaires, trouvées à Pompéi, du carré magique*, Comptes rendus de l'Académie des Inscriptions et Belles Lettres, Paris 1937, pp. 87 ff. and *Osservazioni sull'origine del quadrato magico «Sator Arepo»*, Rendiconti della Pontificia Accademia Romana di Archeologia Ser.3 vol.12 (1936) Roma 1937, pp.401-404. The scholar retracts some views previously held not accepting the interpretation of the letters A and Ω according to the theory of Grosser and Agrell since the Apocalypse of John had not yet been written in 79 C. E. However on this argument see also *Enciclopedia delle Religioni*, vol. 1, Florence 1970, s. v. «Apocalisse di Giovanni», pp. 494-504.

(14) F. Cumont, in: Rendiconti della Pontificia Accademia Romana di Archeologia, Ser.3 vol.13 (1937) Roma 1938, pp. 7-8.

over all the abominations that are committed in it». And to the others I heard Him say: «Follow him, passing through the city and smite; your eye shall not spare and you shall show no pity. Slay old men, young men, youths, girls, young children and women, but slay no one whom you see marked with the tau. And begin at my sanctuary». (Ezekiel 9. 4-6).

«And as I looked there were four wheels, one beside a cherub, the other beside a cherub, and so on, and the appearance of the wheels was-like chrysolite... When they went, they went on their four sides without turning as they went, but in whatever direction the front wheel faced the others followed without turning as they went. And the entire body of the cherubim, their back, hands, wings, and the rims of the wheels, all were full of eyes, all around the four wheels. And I heard these wheels called the whirling ones». (Ezekiel 10. 9, 11-13).

Although the passage of the vision of Ezekiel is not clear most scholars recognize in this vision the glorification of the power of God. The wheels stand for his divine presence which has its seat not only in the Temple at Jerusalem but spreads itself through all the world, so that reaching his followers even in the land where the prisoners suffer, it comforts them in the expectation of their sure liberty (15).

In support of this interpretation important arguments are not lacking. The principal one is the observation that the arrangement of the word *ROTAS* repeated on each side of the square could not better represent the turn of the wheels of the Biblical chariot, wheels which indeed in moving *go round on four sides and in moving do not turn round*:

---

(15) Arguments for a Jewish origin of the magic-square are to be found in H. Fuchs, *Die Erkunft der Satorformel*, Schweizerisches Archiv für Volkskunde, vol. 47, Basel 1951, pp. 28-54.

<table>
<tr><td>R</td><td>O</td><td>T</td><td>A</td><td>S</td></tr>
<tr><td>O</td><td>P</td><td>E</td><td>R</td><td>A</td></tr>
<tr><td>T</td><td>E</td><td>N</td><td>E</td><td>T</td></tr>
<tr><td>A</td><td>R</td><td>E</td><td>P</td><td>O</td></tr>
<tr><td>S</td><td>A</td><td>T</td><td>O</td><td>R</td></tr>
</table>

Fig. 28.
Drawing of the
ROTAS-SATOR

And also in the magic square can be recognized the let-ter T *(tau),* the sign of justice, which can be seen represented in the consonant *t* with which begin and end the two words *tenet,* which intersecting form a cross, which in the ancient Phoenician Samaritan alphabet corresponds to *tau,* the sign of Ezekiel.

De Jerphanion believes that the square arose in a Jewish circle particularly sensitive to the Messianic persuasion, and in a kind of mystic-apologetic literature which flourished round about the time of the first century C. E. When the cryptogram is understood in the light of the prophetic vision of Ezekiel, *Arepo* would be a proper name, the sower of fire, who receives the order from God to enter between the wheels of the chariot, filling his hand with burning charcoal to scatter on the city.

Cumont, on the other hand, who first had the distinc-tion of recognizing the elements of the square in the Biblical passage of the vision of Ezekiel, is of the opinion that the author of the square must have been a Jew converted to Christianity, living perhaps in Italy, and knowing the Latin language. Having disguised in the form of a rebus the thought of the prophet, he believed that he was reflecting the working of the divine plan, whose wheels turning continu-ously are able at the proper time to mark with the tau the forehead of the just moaning in lamentation, but also to strike in the course of their travels the one who has led his life in abomination (16).

3. THE «(C)HRISTIANOS» INSCRIPTION

Mention was previously made of the unusual edifice commonly called the «Hotel of the Christians» (*Regio* VII, xi, 11, 14), where sculptural evidence was found which probably refers to the spirit of irredentism operating in the Jewish community in the course of the Diaspora. But other discoveries, this time epigraphic, merit a separate treatment, for in this building the guests had written on the walls of the rooms. Some of the writing was carefully done with a pointed tool, while other words were written hurriedly with a piece of charcoal. Between the lines, traced with charcoal but

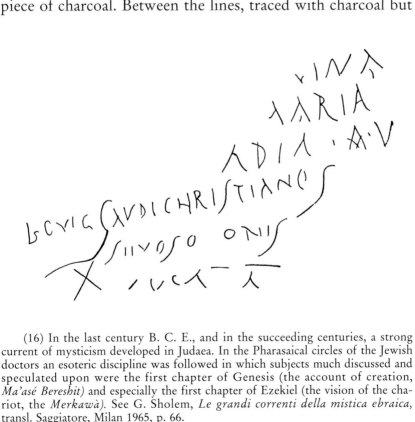

(16) In the last century B. C. E., and in the succeeding centuries, a strong current of mysticism developed in Judaea. In the Pharasaical circles of the Jewish doctors an esoteric discipline was followed in which subjects much discussed and speculated upon were the first chapter of Genesis (the account of creation, *Ma'asé Bereshit*) and especially the first chapter of Ezekiel (the vision of the chariot, the *Merkawà*). See G. Sholem, *Le grandi correnti della mistica ebraica*, transl. Saggiatore, Milan 1965, p. 66.

unfortunately almost vanished, the word *HRISTIAN* or *CHRISTIAN* could be clearly seen. This can be recognized as an allusion to the first Christians and to their growing religion.

The first copy of this singular inscription was made in 1862 by Minervini who went to Pompeii to study it. In the same year Kiessling made a second copy (17). A little later in 1864 De Rossi, having visited the place where it was discovered and seeing only a few traces of the inscription considered it better to insert in the *Bullettino di archeologia cristiana* a drawing he received from Minervini (18).

From that moment this unique document has been the object of continuous and passionate study by scholars who are divided as to their interpretation. Some believe that it was composed of a single text, others on the contrary, that it was formed of two inscriptions. The greater number maintained that an allusion to the Christians was evident; a few on the other hand believe that nothing of this sort can be seen in the inscription (19).

After much effort to make out this enigmatic document, an American scholar, Newbold, arrived at the conclusion that the inscription was Aramaic, written in Latin characters (20). The text thus interpreted, he said, not only reveals an accusation against the Christians and is in keeping with other inscriptions found in the same house (21) but it offers the only possibility of giving clear meaning to the words of the first and the last lines, always difficult for those who held other

(17) *CIL*, IV, 679; A. Kiessling, *Bullettino dell'Istituto di corrispondenza archeologica*, Roma 1862, p. 92.

(18) G. B. De Rossi, *Bullettino di archeologia cristiana*, 2, Roma 1864, pp. 69-72, 95.

(19) For the bibliography see M. Guarducci, *La più antica iscrizione col nome dei Cristiani*, Römische Quartalschrift, vol. 57, 1962, pp. 116-125.

(20) W.R. Newbold, *Five Transliterated Aramaic Inscriptions*, American Journal of Archaeology, Ser. 2, vol. 30, 1926, pp. 291-295, n°. 1.

(21) He alludes to another inscription: *Mulus hic muscelas docuit (CIL,* IV, 2016) which some scholars have considered an indication of the presence of a Christian apostle. See Guarducci, *op. cit.,* 124; Baldi, *op. cit.,* 28.

interpretations. It is however true, the scholar noted, that the Aramaic pronunciation of the inscription differs slightly from the traditional one. But it is necessary to bear in mind that a certain number of Aramaic consonants cannot be represented in Greek or Latin transliterations. In regard to vowel sounds, the Semitic languages, before becoming crystallized, adopted rules which were not always scrupulously followed by the writer and which differed from place to place. In Hebrew and in Aramaic the letters *b, g, d, k, f, t* each have two sounds regulated by some rules which are not for example observed by the Samaritans, and which are observed but often with numerous exceptions in the Syrian language.

In the Pompeian inscriptions we find *v* used in place of *b*, *u* instead of *o*, or vice versa and also the transposition of the *r* before its vowel. This last phenomenon is similar to that which comes to mind in the English language with words of the same root as, for example in «brother» and «brethren», «work» and «wrought».

Accepting then the Aramaic interpretation of the inscription, it would be read thus (22):

The translation would be as follows: «*A strange mind has taken A* (an unknown person who is indicated with this letter) *among the Christians who are holding the man prisoner*».

ב י נ א   א ה ד י י א   ר ד י א ה   א.

ו ד ה י ק   ב ב ן   ד י. CHRISTIANOS.

ע י ח ב ו ש ו   א י נ ש   כ ש ו ח ק

A philological study of the words shows the following: *Vina* = *binà*: «intelligence mind, intellect».

(22) Of the two copies, that of Minervini and the one of Kiessling's, Newbold prefers Minervini's since it agrees with Kiessling's for the first two lines; the rest is somewhat different, but in Aramaic it continues the thought of the first words.

In Daniel (2. 21) we find: *Umandèa leiadeè vinà* «and knowledge is given to those of understanding». Grammatically this feminine substantive when it is not preceded by a word ending in a silent consonant or vowel, as in this case, is pronounced *binà*. The author of the Pompeian inscription should then have adopted the *b* in place of the *v*; but as has been said before the possibility of two sounds for each of the two letters *b, g, d, k, f, t* gave the author a certain freedom.

aaria–aharià = «another, a strange».

Newbold maintains that the traditional reading of this word would be aḥaarià (23) but that with the transposition of the *r* before the vowel *a* and the omission of the following vowel one has *a(ḥ)arià*. We do not understand why the scholar has recourse to this strange explanation. In the *Targum* of Onkelos (Numbers 14. 24) one reads: *Ruaḥ oḥari* in the sense of «a different spirit», in which *oḥari* corresponds exactly to the Pompeian expression *a(ḥ)arià*, where perhaps the final *a* ought to be explained as the influence of the Hebrew on the Aramaic ending of the feminine substantive.

rdia – redia = «has been subjected».

The *e* of *redia* has been omitted, but that should not be surprising because the *shewa*, as the semi-vowel is called, is frequently not indicated in Aramaic. The verb is a third person singular feminine of the perfect and agrees with *binà*. It is however true that in the Palestinian dialect the ending of the perfect would be *at*, but the form in *a* is met with in the Babylonian language and there are often obvious exchanges between the two tongues. At other times the form in *at is* changed to *i* as for example *havai* for *havat*.

vdec – udheq = «and he is driven».

There is first of all a *v* in place of a *u*, this being possible if one bears in mind that the letter *waw* in addition to the sound of the consonant *v* also is given that of the *u* and of the *o*. Moreover the consonant sound of the *waw* varies according to the country. For example, while for the Italian

---

(23) G. Dalman, *Grammatik des Judish Palestinischen Aramaik*, 1905, p. 93.

Jews this corresponded to the latin *v,* for those of India it was pronounced *ue.* Strange, however, is the spelling of the divided word which has its first letter at the end of the third line and continues at the beginning of the fourth line, where the first letter may be read either as *b* or as *d* with a greater incurve on the right for the crossbar of the *e.* One could also object that the final *c* is easily confused with an *o* but it is obvious from the context that this is a verb and, above all, one of motion. The word *deḥeq is* is appropriate. But the fact cannot be denied that the reading of the word is not at all certain.

vigGav – beggav = «in the midst, among».

We have *v* in place of *b,* while the capital *G* is probably only an anticipation of a modern use. Still the double *g* is explicable as due to analogy with the synonym *miggav,* «in the midst».

Newbold does not give an explanation of the first particle *di,* corresponding perhaps to a redundant article governed by *beggav*

siivoso – sheiihbusu = «who are holding».

The Hebrew relative pronoun *she* is not used in Aramaic, which in turn adopted the form *di,* and its presence in this case should be explained as an influence of the Hebrew on the Aramaic. It should also be noted that the *v* in place of the *b,* the ending *oso* in place of *usu* (24) and the lack of the final *n* with which is the correct third-person masculine plural ending in Aramaic reveal clearly the Hebrew influence on the writer's language.

As to the *o* in place of the *u,* it is interesting to note that Minervini suggests that the letters were first written *us* and then changed to *os.* And finally about the pronunciation *sii* rather than *sei,* Dalman notes that the Yemen Jews used *dii* and *lii* in place of *dey* and *ley.*

onis – enish = «the man».

---

(24) For other parallels of this kind see E. A. Speiser, *Secondary Developments in Semitic Phonology,* American Journal of Semitic Languages, vol. 42, Chicago 1926, p. 159.

In Aramaic the word is *enish, enash, nesh,* but the form *onis* is never encountered.

xiuc – kishoq = «as a plaything (prisoner)».

There are some fragments of the third letter which seem to be the arms of a *u,* while the *x* cannot be a cross because early crosses had the T form. The word shows clearly the variations existing in the pronunciation of the two vowel consonant before usage had become crystallized. In the beginning the pronunciation was *cihuq* or also *cshoq;* here instead the writer, since the language was already transformed phonetically, pronounced it *csihuq,* but the grammarians finally placed the vowel after the first consonant, obtaining thus *kishuq* or else *kishoq.*

The interpretation of the Pompeian inscription furnished by the American scholar, as well as those of others who have attempted to explain it, unfortunately still presents numerous difficulties. Only when these are cleared up can the text be established and understood (25).

Two other words, *tiqlof, torgch,* found in the same part of town, under a Latin graffito are recognized by Newbold as Aramaic (26). This reading is acceptable because, besides adding some vowels, which does not present difficulties, the omission of the use of vowels being characteristic of both the Hebrew and Aramaic languages, the only real doubt would consist in changing *or* to *ro.* The two words reconstructed as *tiqlof terogich* refer to an obscenity, but the meaning of the words is in perfect accord with that of the other lines written in Latin.

---

(25) In a new interpretation of this graffito the distinguished Professor Margherita Guarducci also rejects the Aramaic text, and restores instead the Latin: *Bovios audi(t) Christianos sevos osores* («Bovios heeds the Christians, cruel hater»). He relates the attribute *s(a)evos* to the well known accusation of «*haters of the human race*», which was first given by the Romans to the Jews, then transferred to the Christians, since they derived from Jewish stock. He says it is certain that «at Pompeii, before 79, there were some Christians as well as Jews». See Guarducci, *op. cit.,* p. 125.

(26) *CIL,* IV, 760, tav. XVI, 5.

4. The «Cherem» Graffito

We are now in the position of presenting to the attention of scholars and of those who love ancient Pompeii, an interesting and singular document, a graffito quite different from the preceding Hebrew evidence. It appeared in the course of the last excavations in the vestibule of house number 14, *insula* xi region I (formerly II. i.).

This is the first house that you come to on the left when, upon leaving the busy Via dell'Abbondanza, you enter the nar-

Fig. 29. Pompeii, the «cherem» graffito and the stars with five points

row street that divides *insulae* nine and eleven in region one. In this way, by a less congested route, you can reach the quarters near the Grand Palaestra, the ramparts, and the slopes of the Porta Nocera farther on. It is one of those houses which, not being noted for exceptional discoveries, ends up by being neglected by the public and visitors. Modest of plan but not unadorned, it was obviously the home of people in comfortable circumstances who belonged to the Pompeian bourgeoisie.

Here as elsewhere in the city there were restorations and renovations for repairing the damage suffered during the earthquake of 62. The new cover of plaster had not yet been spread on the north wall of the vestibule where at the top of the *zoccolo* there appeared, deeply incised, new evidence giving information about the Pompeian Jews. In the inscription it was possible to read easily the word *cherem*, preceded by another word cut in larger letters which however spelled *poinium* (27). Higher and at the right of the *cherem* two stars with five points were conspicuous, almost equal in size.

It appeared clear that here was the transcription in Latin characters of a Hebrew word but one difficult to interpret, because of the lack of a context to aid in understanding the exact meaning.

There is the additional fact that the consonant group *ch* can be the transcription in the Eastern tongues of two different Hebrew consonants, the *ḥet* and the *caf,* so that the term *cherem* can correspond to two Hebrew words *ḥerem* or *cherem,* the one beginning with *ḥet,* the other with *caf* (28).

It is necessary also to note that the verbal root *ḥrm* is not found in the entire area of the Semitic West which includes the languages spoken along the coast of Africa up to Carthage. This, added to other arguments which are presen-

---

(27) The inscription of the Cherem, together with that of the Magic-Square, has been placed in the Antiquarium at Pompeii. Cfr. C. Giordano – I. Kahn, *Il Cherem biblico in Pompei antica,* Rendiconti dell'Accad. di Archeologia Lettere e BB. AA. di Napoli N.S. 49 (1974) Napoli 1975, pp. 167-176.

(28) In the word *ḥerem* the *h* has a strongly aspirated sound as the German *ch,* while in the word *cherem* the *ch* is pronounced as a hard *c.* It is however true that in the Vulgate, the consonant *caf* is rendered with *ch,* and the consonant *het* with the simple *h* but in the texts prior to this before the fourth century, the two previously mentioned consonants are variously transcribed even in the course of the same text. See *Vetus latina, Confronti interlineari tra la versione di S. Girolamo, quella dei Settanta ed altre antiche versioni della Bibbia,* vol. 1, Freiburg 1951; *Codex Palimpsestus, Antiquissimae Veteris Testamenti translationis latinae fragmenta,* 1885, where Hebrew words are transcribed with the latin alphabet. For a scientific treatment of *ḥerem* see A. Fernández, *El herem bíblico,* Biblica, vol. 5, Roma 1924, pp. 3-25; L. Del Porte, *L'Anathème de Jahvè,* Recherches de Science Religieuse, vol. 5, Paris 1914, pp. 297-338.

ted in the course of this chapter, makes it certain that this word belongs only to the Hebrew language (29).

But the diverse interpretations possible require that the solution must be furnished not only by the history and the laws of the Jewish people, but also by the aid of Hebrew philology.

ḤEREM

The Hebrew root *ḥerem* is found, however, in other equally strong words which are close not only to words that characterize Arab customs, but also those of other Semitic peoples. The *root ḥrm* includes the idea of separation and restriction of use. Separation and reserved use are described in two Arabic words of the same root.

One is expressed by the term *ḥaram* which means «to exclude, to render inaccessible». In the large inscription at Petra the tomb and its two dependencies are *vḥrg* and *ḥrm* to Dusare the god of Nabatea. This association of terms underlines at the same time the sacred character and also makes clear the idea of prohibition and of reservation (30). It should not be forgotten that among ancient peoples the concepts of sacredness and impurity, while in some respects opposite, are in other respect connected. An impure, abhorred object, becomes set apart from common use to make sure that no one by touching it is contaminated, while a sacred object, pleasing to God, is likewise set apart because it is reserved for divine use. The one and the other, although so dif-

(29) See J. Hoffjitzer, *Dictionnaire des Inscriptions Semitiques de l'Ovest*, s.v. «Herem».

(30) De Yogus, *Inscription nabatéenne de Petra*, Revue Biblique, vol.4, 1895, pp. 281-288 ; M. J. Lagrange, *Notre exploration à Petra*, Revue Biblique, vol. 6, 1897, p. 223.

ferent, are really *herem;* an object can be set apart from common use for two reasons, so that it will not contaminate if impure, or be contaminated (31) if pure.

It is known that *Hermon* was a sacred mountain (32) and that its sides were covered with many temples. The discoveries in the south of Arabia have restored to the term *ḥrm* the meaning of sanctuary, and to the word *bḥrm* the meaning of being set apart. The Bible itself explains the name of the city of Hormah with *herem* (that which is destroyed).

> «And the Lord hearkened to the voice of Israel and gave over the Canaanites to them and they destroyed them and their cities in the manner of *herem* to the name of this place was called *Hormah*» (Numbers 21. 3).

And lastly, with respect to the root *ḥrm* in the Chaldean language, the serpent is always indicated by the name of *ḥurman* since his bite being incurable rendered the person *herem* (33).

The second word that signifies with the same root the idea of reserved use is the word *ḥarim* (in Assyrian, *ḥarimtu*), that is the *ḥarem,* the gynaeceum, or women's apartment in the house, which was inaccessible to every one except the master. The analogies do not stop at this point because *ḥaram,* as the *ḥarim,* designates the enclosure which contains the things inaccessible to the profane, the best known being the urban *ḥaram* of Jerusalem. In the sanctuary of Petra the access to the *ḥaram* is simply indicated by two obelisks, which recall the Yaḥin and Bo'as (34) raised on each side of the door of the Temple of Jerusalem, which is a true *ḥaram.*

---

(31) See W. R. Smith, *Lectures on the Religion of the Semites,* London 1907, p. 159 ff.

(32) Jerome, *De situ et nominibus locorum hebraicorum,* s. v. «Hermon»; Deuteronomy 3.8.

(33) J. Buxtorf, *Lexicon chaldaicum talmudicum et rabbinicum,* Basel 1639, pp. 827-829, s. v. «Ḥerem», «Ḥurman».

(34) I. Sam. 7. 21.

In the Bible from the verbal roots *ḥrm* is derived the substantive *ḥerem* (the modern transcription prefers the form *cherem*). For various reasons, not to be discussed here, this word is used with two meanings, depending upon whether a thing becomes forbidden and condemned to total destruction because abhorred by God, or whether being pleasing to Him it is set apart from common use and designated for His service. There are thus two classes of *ḥerem: 1) ḥerem* for execration, and 2) *ḥerem* for sacrifice.

1) *Ḥerem* for execration, or in the modern exegesis warlike *ḥerem*, always strikes cruelly persons or things which one considered contaminated. Because what is forbidden is abominable in the eyes of the divinity, all those things are objects of his wrath and therefore condemned to destruction which is fulfilled in obedience to God:

«The city and as many as are in it will be *ḥerem* to God» (35).

A terrifying example of *ḥerem* for execration is that against the Amalekites and their king Agag. In the name of God, Samuel ordered Saul to fight the idolatrous Amalekites, who had oppose the entry into Israel during the Exodus:

«Now go and smite Amalek and destroy in the manner of *ḥerem* everything which he has, without sparing anything. Put do death everything: men and women, children and sucklings, oxen and sheep, camels and asses» (36).

At Ai (Joshua. 10, 1) at Hazor (Joshua. 11, 11), and still other places God appeared, always watching over his people, almost always imposing war, intervening in an efficacious manner, and demanding every time the *ḥerem* by means of his intervention. Often to the horror of slaughter was added that of fire, as happened at Jericho.

(35) Joshua 6. 17.
(36) I. Sam. 15. 13.

«And they destined to *ḥerem* all that were in
the city, passing through the edge of the sword men,
women, young and old, oxen, sheep and asses...».

«They burned then the city and everything that
it contained, sparing only the silver, gold, the vessels
of bronze and of iron...» (37).

Another time the *ḥerem* of execration was ordered in
the Bible not only against the idolatrous population which
inhabited pre-Israelite Palestine and with whom the Jews
clashed, but it was invoked against the Israelites themselves
who were guilty of apostasy:

«Strike all the inhabitants of that city. Put them
to the edge of the sword. Destroy in the manner of
ḥerem together with all those who are within, and
its cattle, putting them to the edge of the sword».

«And gather the spoils of the city in the middle
of the square, and burn the city completely and all
its spoils with fire, for the Lord your God» (38).

The same treatment then was applied to the belongings
of the idolaters:

«Burn with fire the sculptures of their gods. Do
not covet the silver or the gold which will be on
them... and do not take into your house abominable
things, which should be treated as *ḥerem*» (39).

It is categorically stated:

«Whoever sacrifices to the gods should be treated as *ḥerem*» (40).

Ḥerem then for execration which is encountered in the
Yahwh and Elohim documents always evokes a series of terrible episodes in which fire plays an important part, and in

(37) Joshua 6. 21, 24.
(38) Deut. 13. 15, 16.
(39) Deut. 7. 25, 26.
(40) Exodus 22. 20.

94

which the wrath of the God of Israel is applied with extreme rigour against his enemies. It also appears clear that the first cause of *ḥerem* with which God punishes persons or orders the destruction or a thing is the practice of idolatry or the serving of it in some way.

But things taken away can also be pleasing to God, for which he has a second class of *ḥerem:*

2) *Ḥerem* for sacrifice, or irrevocable consecration to the service of the divinity of an object with which he is pleased, becomes after the renunciation of the owner set apart so that it will not be contaminated, but will be irrevocably destined to the cult. This type of *ḥerem* in modern terminology is said to be *ḥerem de offerenda.*

In the Bible, in treating of sacrifice, the price for the redemption of what is consecrated to the Lord is fixed, save however for two exceptions which cannot be redeemed by an offering or bought from a priest. The first exception regards the first-born of some species of animals which as such belongs to God.

«But no one may dedicate something first-born
to the Lord either ox, or sheep, or what it may be,
for it already belongs to the Lord».

The other exception are those things that have been consecrated by a vow, and so cannot be redeemed or bought:

«But no thing consecrated for *ḥerem* that a man
has consecrated to the Lord of all that is his,
whether of men, or of beasts, or of fields which he
inherited, shall be sold or redeemed. Every *ḥerem is*
a very sacred thing belonging to the Lord» (41).

What is done with such a *ḥerem* is not said, however it is evident that it was not always destroyed in honour of God, for even if the animals could be offered in sacrifice this would not be true of the fields which are mentioned. These

(41) Leviticus 27. 26 ff.

could be used either for the maintenance of the cult, or for the support of its ministers.

> «They shall eat the offerings of cereal and the sacrifices for sin and guilt; and likewise every *ḥerem* thing in Israel shall be theirs (of the priests)» (42).

Which then of the two meanings of the word *ḥerem* is to be understood if the inscription is to be taken in a Biblical context? Without doubt the formula of *ḥerem* for sacrifice is possible, the word having been written as a vow of consecration. The person, as one repeating an ancestral rite, wished to consecrate the house to God making it a thing sacred to him.

Similarly the other interpretation of *ḥerem* for execration is possible; then the word would be a curse hurled in a spirit of revenge by a Jew against the city which had seen the suffering of his slavery. He in the ruinous spread of ashes and of fire saw manifest the sentence of God on the people of the oppressors.

In addition to these two interpretations, which although different are reducible to a single fundamental idea which is derived from «setting apart», the word *cherem* could also have a third interpretation.

CHEREM

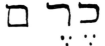

By changing the first consonant to *caf* in place of *ḥet* the Pompeian expression could be the transliteration of the Hebrew word *cherem* with the meaning of «vineyard». This word is found in this sense in the account of the universal flood:

> «The sons of Noaḥ who went forth from the ark were Shem, Ḥam, and Japeth.

(42) Ezekiel 44. 29.

96

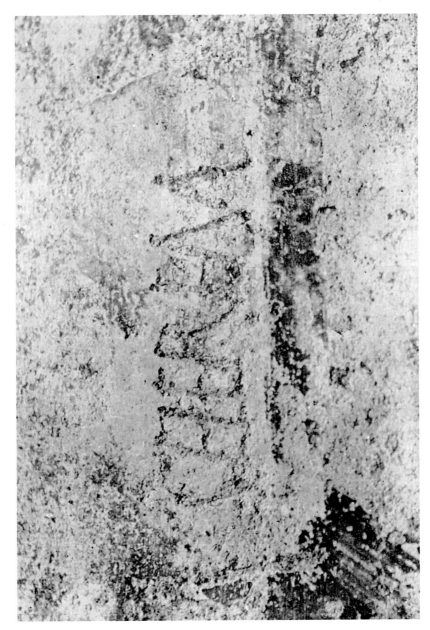

Fig. 30. Cherem

97

These were the sons of Noaḥ; from these came the population of the entire earth. Noaḥ, the farmer, was the first to plant a vineyard» (43).

Later in prophetic literature the vineyard frequently became the symbol of the Jewish people, as in the splendid parable of the «Vineyard of the Lord» of which God was the careful proprietor (44):

> «For the vineyard of the Lord of hosts
>   is the house of Israel;
> the men of Judah
>   are his pleasant plant...» (45).

The image was natural for people who considered the epitome of well-being to rest tranquilly in the shade of their own vine and under their own fig tree (46).

It is especially interesting to point out here that the school founded by a disciple of Hillel, Rabban Joḥanan ben Zaccai, was known by the title of «Vineyard». It said in fact that Rabban Joḥanan ben Zaccai while the Sanctuary was in flames decided in that tragic moment to save the most precious patrimony of Israel, her Tradition. By virtue of a clever stratagem he managed to bring it about that Vespasian, who having recognized him, welcomed him benignly and granted him permission to found a scholarly academy at Jahvnè, the ancient Jamnia. So this insignificant city in the Philistine plain along the Mediterranean, between the maritime cities of Japho and Ashdod, became a religious and national centre destined to gather the immense Jewish spiritual patrimony which was then arranged into the Mishna and in the Talmud. The students who were assembled here from far and wide were so numerous, enthusiastic, and disciplined that they seemed like religious shoots of the vine, and for this reason

---

(43) Genesis 9. 18.
(44) Jeremiah 2. 21; Matthew 21. 33-34.
(45) Isaiah 5. 7.
(46) I Kings 5. 5; Micah 4. 4; Zach. 3. 10.

the school was called *cherem Jahvnè*, «*The Vineyard of Jahvnè*» (47).

In this sense the *cherem* of the inscription could be understood as the name of the Jewish community at Pompeii, or as an indication of a nascent academic and religious group which would be no more lacking here than in other cities inhabited by Jews who had formerly been slaves and then freedmen. Of this group Fabius Eupor, in the last years, was the chief spokesman in the guise of *princeps libertinorum*.

5. THE STAR WITH FIVE POINTS

The motif of the star with five points appears in Israel on a terra-cotta vase of fifth century B.C.E. containing the tribute to be sent to the Persian empire; between the five points of the star there is the legend in ancient Hebrew, *Jesushalem*, while on the other face one reads *Yehud*, the official name of South Judaea during the Persian period (48).

It is indeed difficult to go back to the origins of the symbolic significance attributed to the geometric figure of the pentaculum or star with five points, which one finds described in the *esotericmagic* literature of numerous peoples as an amulet endowed with special power (49).

In both Jewish post-Biblical literature and in the Arabic authors (50) there is the legend of a special seal-ring which King Solomon had received as a gift from Heaven, a ring given magic powers, among them that of exorcising evil spirits. However from its description some say that it had the form of a star with six points rather than that of a pentaculum (51).

---

(47) *Talmud Bava Batra,* chap. 8, 131; *Talmud Ketubot,* chap. 4, 49; Alfredo Toaff, *Commento all'Agadà di Pasqua,* Florence 1949, p. 13.

(48) Ezra 5. 1. For a discussion see *Encyclopedia Miqrait,* Jerusalem 1958, s. v. «Tevihot Jerusalem».

(49) E. Levi, *Histoire de la Magie,* Paris 1860, p. 450 ff.

(50) Lane, *Arabian Night's Entertainments,* chap. XX, n. 93.

(51) For the legend of the seal-ring of Solomon see also *Talmud Ghittin* 68; *Tanhuma Ha-Qadom;* N. N. Bialik and J. H. Ravnitzky, *Sefer Ha-hagadà,* vol. 1, Tel Aviv 1960, p. 97 ff.

It is evident then that among the Jewish people there were two symbols, the *Maghen David,* or shield of David having the form of a star with six points, and the *Tabahat or Hotam Shelomo,* or seal-ring of Solomon having the form of a star with five points. In popular belief these two symbols were considered protective emblems, also as simple ornamental architectural motifs. This was the significance of the star with five points – with a geometrical design identical to the Pompeian one – found in the ancient Synagogue of Tell-Hum at Caphernaum on the north bank of Lake of Gennesaret near the Jordan (52).

Of the two emblems, the *Maghen David* (53) prevailed in time and became the most widely used symbol of the Jews. Today it appears in a white field enclosed by two blue bands in the flag of the restored State of Israel.

The Jews, with their sublimely spiritual concept of a God who did not permit images of Himself, were opposed in general to the official acceptance of symbols. So it is understandable that the *Maghen David* and the *Tabahat* or *Hotam Shelomo* are almost ignored in the rabbinical literature. Nothing precise is known of their original significance but probably these astral symbols, whether they were in the form of a pentaculum, or were derived from the combination of two equilateral triangles, were related in some way to that inextinguishable vein of Messianic hope which in every period has sustained the expectations of the oppressed and per-

(52) The star with five points also appears sometimes as an ornamental motif in the decorations in synagogues and cathedrals, such as those at Brandenburg, and at Stendal. See *The Jewisk Encyclopedia, s.v.* «Solomon's seal», vol. 8, p. 252.

(53) It seems that in Italy, the first *Maghen David* was found at Tarentum on a tomb of the third century. See M. Herbert *Adler,* in: «J.Q.R.», vol. 14, 1924. One of the first Jewish documents to mention this symbol is *Eshkol Ha-Kofer* by Jehudà Hadassi of the twelfth century. For the prehistoric representations of the *pentaculum* and hexagram in some caves of Southern France, the Iberian Peninsula and Sardinia, see A. Glory, *Gravures rupestres schématiques dans l'Ariege,* in: Gallia-Fouilles et Monuments Archéologiques en France Métropolitaine, vol. 5, Paris 1947, n. 1, pp. 1-45; G. Spano, *Pentacoli, ossia amuleti in oro, argento e bronzo,* Bullettino Archeologico Sardo, vol. 10, 1864, p. 140; A. G. Segre, *Segnalazioni di graffiti rupestri in Sardegna,* Extract from *Studi Sardi,* vol. 14-15 (1955-57) Sassari 1957, pp. 3-7.

secuted Jews. For centuries, on the most diverse shores, perhaps they had concealed in these symbols their longing for a return to Jerusalem and to the vision of a time so much longed for by the distant progeny, in which:

«A star shall be born from Jacob
And a sceptre will be raised from Israel» (Numbers 14, 17).

6. POINIUM

The word *poinium,* which was written in large letters in front of the word *cherem,* deserves a further note. We are indebted to Professor M. Guarducci for the valuable suggestion that *poinium* could be the Latin form of a Greek noun ending in *nion,* namely *poimnion,* meaning «flock».

One might also see Biblical symbolism in this word. If the unknown writer of the inscription in the room at Pompeii used the terminology of Isaiah, the symbol of the Vine of the Lord, to describe the people of Israel (for the word *cherem* can be interpreted this way, see *supra* pp. 96-99), with the word *poinium,* meaning flock, he may also have borrowed another figure no less beautiful from the same prophet. By this symbol, used in both the Old Testament (Isaiah 49. 9; Jeremiah 23. 3; Ezekiel 43. 2 ff.; Psalms 78. 52, 80. 2, 95. 7; Micah 2. 12 ff. etc.) and in the New Testament (Matthew 18. 12 ff.; Luke 15. 3-7; John 10. 1-10) the people of Israel are described as a flock, of which God is the loving shepherd. He brings back his flock to the sheepfold, or makes them to pass through high places, guiding with equal love the large numbers of his people in foreign lands:

«He shall feed his flock like a shepherd,
he shall gather the lambs with his arm» (Isaiah 40, 11).

But in addition to this valuable suggestion, the authors see another possible meaning in the word *poinium.* In the Greek language, so familiar to the Jews of the Diaspora, we

Fig. 31. Poinium and Cherem

102

find the word *poiné,* similar in meaning to the Latin word *poena.* Both of these would correspond to the other meaning of the word *cherem,* which as we have seen *(supra* pp. 93-95) can also mean pain, punishment, or destruction. The word *poinium* could then be a Latin form of the Greek word *poiné* and refer to the last dramatic moments of the city, as does the inscription of Sodom and Gomorrah.

Regardless of the interpretation one accepts, it is impossible not to recognize the strange connection whether only symbolic, or synonymous, between the two words which are clearly not different, but related. This would give the scholar the first Pompeian evidence of a bilingual Hebrew-Greek (in Latin letters) document.

7. A Greek Graffito Referring to Genesis

In conclusion it is not possible to omit two inscriptions alluding to Genesis (54), conceived as the grand book of creation. The Greek graffiti in Latin characters:

MEGISTE GENESIS and GENESIS

should be taken in this sense rather than seeing in it an allusion to a nomen or cognomen *Genesius.*

---

(54) *CIL,* IV, 4300, 4321. Pompei, *Regio* V, *Ins.* V, n. 3.

CHAPTER VI

POST – ERUPTION BIBLICAL VOICES

A little time after the catastrophe some survivors making their way over the spent cinders directed their steps toward buried Pompeii. From the deep covering of cinders the tops of the public buildings stood out, as well as the roofs of houses that had been inhabited only a short time before. These were precious signs for the vanguard of the pillagers who hoped to recover domestic and artistic objects. They were able to do this, sometimes at great risk, by locating well known patrician houses and digging down shafts (1).

Some of the survivors paused for a moment on top of the noble house of the «Golden Amorini» which, as we have said, belonged to a branch of the *Poppaea gens*, related by way of Sabina to the emperor Nero. Exploration was carried out in the peristyle of this house, still today one of the most delightful in the city, with its statuettes, marble portraits and the other works of art which adorn it. Modern excavators noticed that a statue had been removed from the pool of the garden and carried away already *ab antiquo* (2).

During their search the explorers found themselves also in the vestibule of this house. One of them, on the plaster of the walls, marked observations and comments regarding the terrible events which a little before had afflicted the region.

---

(1) For the exploration of Pompeian buildings in ancient times see G. Fiorelli, *Descrizione di Pompei*, Napoli 1875, p. 109 ff.; *CIL*, IV, 2311, M. Della Corte, *I M. Lorei Tiburtini di Pompei*, Atti della Società Tiburtina di Storia ed Arte, vol.11, 1931-32, pp. 182-216; Id., *Esplorazioni di Pompei immediatamente successive alla catastrofe dell'anno 79*, In memoria di Vasile Pârvan, Bucarest 1934, pp. 96-109.
(2) A. Sogliano, *Notizie degli Scavi*, 1906, p. 374.

Fig. 32. Pompeii, House of the Golden Amorini. Peristyle

Photo Ander.

The observations, although with a different viewpoint, are near to the thought of the epigram of Martial written eight years after the catastrophe. In this he lamented the miserable lot of the Vesuvian city and contrasted the florid life of yesterday with the sad desolation of today (3).

The metrical inscriptions, product of a mind not unlearned, were probably written by a single hand. They are still visible on the walls of the vestibule; some are on the wall to the right, others on the wall that is to the left as you enter the house. The first gives us the following hexameter:

Quinquaginta ubi erant (adsunt) exinde iacent (4)

(3) *Ep.*, IV, 44.
(4) *CIL*, IV, 6819. For the interpretation of this graffito see M. Della Corte, *Le più remote esplorazioni di Pompei. Nuovi contributi allo studio su Pompei ed i Cristiani*, Historia, vol. 8, Milano 1934, n.2, pp. 354-372; Id, *Case ed abitanti in Pompei*, p. 58 ff.

QVINRO GI GIINTX

YBIILSNT

IIX INDII ISCIINT

This is perfectly explainable when one thinks that in groping about the house the explorers must have happened upon numerous bodies of the unfortunate and formerly powerful inhabitants of this place. The thought of the verse is clear «From then, the fifty lie here». In other words, from the day that they were overcome by the catastrophe they lie here dead – the fifty inhabitants of the house.

Two other inscriptions, when properly joined together, form a distich:

Sis Cotini voto post fata novissima (poclum)
quo bibet pellex saxa cinique tegunt (5)

SICCOTINIVOTO POSTATA NOVISSIMA

QVO BIBUTPIIAIIX SASSA CINI SUIIIITIGUNT

The fierce invective can be translated: «Thus, according to the vow of Cotinus, after the very recent cataclysm, stones and ashes now cover the cup with which he was making libations to the adulteress». Who the Cotinus was that is described in the verse as a prophet of misfortune, is not given us to know with certainty. But the adulteress who was drinking from the cup can be recognized as Poppea, an inhabitant of the house, perhaps the very person whose beautiful marble portrait still remains in the peristyle (6).

(5) *CIL*, IV, 6820, 6825.
(6) For the iconography of the garden see A. de Franciscis, *Il ritratto romano in Pompei*, Naples 1951, p. 23 ff.

The symbolism of the prostitute and the cup lying under stones and ashes is indeed original, devised in the apocalyptic background of the Pompeian desolation, but it is not new and is of the kind that is alluded to in the Biblical imagery. The figure comes very close to the imagery of the prophet Ezekiel in which he represented Jerusalem in the guise of the adulteress Oholibah in the act of drinking from a precious cup, being led full of drunkenness, her eyes out of focus, until she would be judged, put in confusion, and her house burned with fire (7). Another use of the motif of the cup is found in Jeremiah where, in speaking of the sins and sufferings of Jerusalem, the prophet apostrophizes for her corrupt life the city of Edom who also has become drunk from a cup so that God will punish her iniquity (8).

In the Sacred Scriptures the divine wrath is always prophesied with the image of the chalice from which the adulteress drinks, as is the destruction which would strike the nation represented in the garments of such a woman. The cup represents only the instrument of divine wrath and not the chalice of pleasure. But how close is the Biblical image to the Pompeian verses!

In the first the figure of a prophet prophesying sorrow dominates. In the second there is clearly mentioned the mysterious Cotinus who likewise prophesies dire events after they had already happened. Just as in the vision of the Biblical prophet total destruction came upon the city marked by God, so here in the poetic language of the inscription, as on the other side of the chalice, stones and ashes give tragic testimony of a total extermination (9).

And lastly from the verification of the total destruction of a hated world the unknown writer of the inscription goes

---

(7) Ezekiel 23, 32.
(8) Jeremiah 25. 12. For the symbolism of the cup in the Old Testament see A. Condamin, *Jeremie*, 1963, p. 340.
(9) For Cotinus, a probable Christian, and head of a band of Christians see M. Della Corte, *Case ed abitanti in Pompei*, p. 113; P. Ciprotti, *Conoscere Pompei*, Rome 1959, p. 61.

108

on to postulate the vision of two groups of people divided among themselves, attacking each other:

Sol gelidam contra firmat plaquideam gentem (10).

)9ト Ѵ II Ⴑ)ʎ ᏟᴏɴᎢᴧᎩ ᴦ\ᴧᴧᎴᎢ ᴘḺᴧǫᴠɴᴧᴧᴧ ᏟᴧᴧᎢᴧ

«Against the frozen peoples, the sun strengthens the people who are pleasing to God».

Some scholars feel that even if it is not clearly stated, there should be no doubt about seeing in the frozen peoples the pagans who remain indifferent to the teachings of the new faith; the people who are pleasing to God would be the Christians (11).

But one cannot deny, on the other hand, that the inscription might be the thoughts of a person who had been saved from the Pompeian slaughter. In fact, the superstitious pillager of the house, coming from time to time upon the numerous bodies of the victims frozen by death, would have concluded that since he had survived such a great calamity he must truly be among those who were pleasing to God, who was symbolized by the sun which was given to those whom the divinity protected, while it was taken away from the dead. In this case, the graffito would concern only the final event at Pompeii and would refer only to this city.

However if one believes that in the preceding verses there is a definite gnomic air and thought which seems to take its origin from Cotinus, there is no reason why one might not also see such an inspiration in this verse so that it too could easily fit into a Biblical context.

The vision of the two worlds in conflict, even if one does not presuppose necessarily that Cotinus was a Christian or a Jew approaching Christianity, could be connected with the

(10) *CIL,* IV, 6821.
(11) M. Della Corte, *Case ed abitanti in Pompei,* p. 64; *I Cristiani a Pompei,* Rendiconti dell'Accad. di Archeol. Lettere e Belle Arti di Napoli, N.S. 19 (1938-39) Napoli 1939, p. 10.

proposals of the Sibylline Oracle. In the fourth book known of course to be a genuine Jewish document are recounted to the people of God, pleasing to Him, the catastrophes which will overtake Rome, and the other nations which have persecuted the people of God. In the Sibylline Oracle the circumlocution of «pious men» is used to indicate the Jewish people (12). Reference is made to the recent mis-fortunes of Israel; in addition the book adopts an anti-Roman, and more generally, an anti-pagan spirit. The following warning which ties in with the Pompeian verses is clearly stated:

> «The impious will then be sunk in the infernal abyss, while all the pious men will be restored to life on earth, through the divine grace *in the sweet light of the sun*; blessed are those who will live in that time» (13).

The contrast between two worlds, the one illuminated and heated by the sun, the other immersed in obscurity and ice, is found again in the dualism of the light and the darkness, one of the beliefs of that distant Jewish community of the *Qumran* to which belong the famous Dead Sea Scrolls which speak of the War of the Sons of Light against the Sons of Darkness (14).

The Pompeian expression *plaquidea* finds an indirect parallel in one of the so-called Psalms of Gratitude which seem to have been part of the liturgy of this sect. In the seventh Psalm one reads:

«Those who are *pleasing* to You will remain in your presence forever».

The expression, «those who are approved by God», or «who are pleasing to God», also has a very solid base resting

---

(12) IV. 132, 133. For the chronology of the books of the Oracle read Geffcken, *Komposition und Entstehungszeit der Oracula Sibillina*, Leipzig 1902; and more recently, Rzach in *Real Encyclopädie der classichen Altertumswissenschaft*, 2 serie, II, 2, 2103, s.v. «Sibyllinische Orakel».

(13) IV, 178, 190

(14) M. Burrows, *Prima di Cristo. La scoperta dei rotoli del Mar Morto*, Milano 1958, p. 404.

on various passages of sacred Scripture. In Ecclesiastes we have these verses:

> «For God giveth to a man that is good in his sight wisdom, and knowledge, and joy: but to the sinner he giveth travail, to gather and to heap up, that he may give to him that is good before God ....» (15).

Now the Vulgate translates the Hebrew expression «he who is pleasing to Him», with *qui placuit Deo*. This expression is found in Wisdom (4. 10) with *placens Deo factus est dilectus*, in Psalms (68. 32) with *qui placuit Deo*, in Baruch (4. 14) and in Ecclesiasticus (41. 16) with *Henoch placuit Deo*. A variant reading with *placere Domino* is found in Psalms (114. 19) and in Proverbs (16. 7 and 21. 4).

Moreover the word *placuideus*, derived by joining the word *placere* with the word *Deus*, in addition to finding some predecessors in the oriental name of the type, *Abdeus*, finds its successors in those of Christian Africa with *Quotvultdeus, Habetdeus, Deusdat, Deusdedit*, and still others (16). Although these are later than the second century, they must certainly have had predecessors in the earlier period which is cloaked in documentary obscurity.

The expression is also found in the New Testament in the first letter to the Thessalonians (2, 15):

> «they killed the Lord Jesus, and his prophets, and drove us out, and *are not pleasing to God* and are adverse to all men».

The collision of two worlds so powerful and menacing, that of the *frozen people,* and of the others *who are pleasing to God,* is also found in the Gospels. The Pompeian inscription with its vision of the peoples confronting each other repeats very nearly the sermon on the fullness of time in Luke, where one reads:

---

(15) Ecclesiastes 2. 26.
(16) For what has been said see M. Della Corte, *Le più remote esplorazioni di Pompei*, Historia vol.8, Milano 1934.

«One people will rise up against another people, and one kingdom against another» (17).

This parallelism is more noticeable if the verse is read in its context, where it is said:

«In every place there, will be great earthquakes, and famine, and pestilence, and there will be also some frightful prodigies and some great signs from heaven» (18).

Most of this had happened in the area around Vesuvius. The Pompeian document in this sense could be truly understood as the most ancient and venerable evidence of a proto-Christian period at Pompeii, a period characterized by the contrast between the pagan world and the Christian one.

The discovery of the *Cherem* inscription flanked by the two symbols of the star with five points of *Hotam Shelomo is* definite evidence for the presence of the Jews in Pompeii and answers understandable reservations recently held (19). There is no doubt about the existence of a Jewish colony in the Vesuvian city, whose members comprised every social class, from those of humble servile condition to those of comfortable freedman status. Some had become prosperous in business and active in politics. Some of the freedmen even had servants of their own.

The relations between the Jews and the indigenous element at Pompeii begin to appear clear, and indicate a situation of friction (20). Sentiments of scorn were expressed either through the word «circumcised» with an offensive intent, or by artistic expressions such as the Judgment of Solomon, the story of Jonah, the pastry-cook statuette, or the Jew of the Shield. One reacts with less acrimony to the inscription of Sodom and Gomorrah, to that of the *Cherem*

(17) Luke 21. 10.
(18) Luke 21. 11.
(19) P. Brezzi in A. Baldi, *La Pompei cristiano-giudaica*, Cava dei Tirreni 1964, Introduction, p. XXVIII.
(20) See Baldi, *op. cit.*, 85.

if this was intended in the sense of anathema, and to the statuette on the kettle-lid.

If on the other hand the word *cherem* points out the little room in which the few Israelites in the city assembled on special occasions, a group for whom Fabius Eupor was in the last period the chief spokesman, thus explaining his attribute of *princeps libertinorum,* then to this group *(Ckerem)* could be assigned the inscription of the magic square. Because of its use of the Latin language and its reference to things anachronistic for this period, it is doubtful if the magic square had hidden Christian significance. But it is possible it reveals activity in a Jewish setting (21) especially encouraged by the great stream of the theology of the *Ma' ase Bereshit* and of the *Merkava,* that is, the mystic speculation about the first chapter of Genesis and the vision of the Heavenly throne-chariot in the first chapter of Ezekiel.

Jewish environment also showed itself not indifferent, as in the two other maritime ports of Pozzuoli and Alexandria, to the influence of the *impulsore Chresto* and to early Christian propaganda. Alexandria already had as its bishop the Jew Ananius who spread propaganda publicly in the synagogue and in Jewish circles, so that Claudius did not hesitate to warn against «that pestilence now menacing all the civil world» (τῆς οἰκουμένης νόσος) (22).

The fact then that the term *Christianos* was found in a place known through other interesting discoveries to be connected with the Jews, and even more the inscription in the House of the Golden Amorini should confirm the view of a scholar who has said:

---

(21) For the anachronism of the magic square, see P. Brezzi in Baldi, *op. cit.,* Introduction, XXIX. Among numerous other scholars who treated of Jewish mysticism in the last centuries B. C. E., see G. Sholem, *Le grandi correnti della mistica ebraica,* Milano 1965, chap. II and also Sh. Spiegel, *Journal of Biblical Literature,* vol. 54, 1935, pp. 164-165.

(22) For the documentation see W. Seston, *L'Empereur Claude et les Chretiens,* Revue d'Histoire et de Philosophie Religieuses, 1931, n. 31; G. De Sanctis, *Rivista di Filosofia ed Istruzione Classica,* 1924, p. 473; S. Reinach, *Revue Archéologique,* Paris 1924, p. 230; 1925, p. 171 and 1927, p. 276.

«It is not denied that these Jews (of Pompeii) may have given life to a Judeo-Christian community, one of those primitive forms of Christianity in which evangelical elements were intertwined and blended with the ancient prophetic and rabbinical tradition, because such was precisely the first phase of the Christian cult» (23).

If this then was the case it was perhaps in the cenaculum of the *Cherem*, in meetings inspired by Judaism and the ritual of the synagogue, that there were some inspired by the message of the *impulsore Chresto*. Among these perhaps was Cotinus whose concepts of struggle might seem to reflect the intransigence of Judaism more than calm Christian spirituality (24), but only if one forgets that the rise of Christianity greatly accentuated the conflict between the pagan world and the converted world:

«Do you believe that I have come to bring peace to the earth? No, I say to you, but rather division» (25).

The discovery of the *cherem* renders this interpretation very likely if not certain. There was at Pompeii almost certainly, as past and recent discoveries relating to the Jews show, a close relationship and rapport between Judaism and Christianity, both extraordinary expressions of human religiosity, both constituting the greater part of the moral and spiritual patrimony of modern civilization.

(23) This is the wise conclusion of Baldi, *op. cit.,* 73.
(24) We disagree with what is said by Baldi, *op. cit.,* 83.
(25) Luke 12. 51.

BIBLIOGRAPHY

(Cfr. GARCIA Y GARCIA L. *Nova Bibliotheca Pompeiana*, Roma 1998, vol. 2, pp. 1330-1331)

BALDI Agnello, *La Pompei giudaico-cristiana*. (Pref. di Paolo Brezzi). Cava dei Tirreni (Di Mauro Ed.) 1964.

L'anatema e la croce. Ebrei e cristiani in Pompei antica. (Pref. di Paolo Brezzi). Cava dei Tirreni (Di Mauro Ed.) 1983.

CAMMILLIERI Rino, *Il Quadrato Magico. Un mistero che dura da duemila anni*. Milano (Rizzoli) 1999.

CARCOPINO Jérôme, *Études d'histoire chrétienne*. Paris 1953 (2. éd., Paris 1963).

CATALANO Virgilio, *Case, abitanti e culti di Ercolano*. Annali del Pontificio Istituto superiore di scienze e lettere «S. Chiara» 13, Napoli 1963, pp. 213-342 (spec. pp. 307 e 341 segg. for the Jews in Herculaneum. Is forthcoming the new edition, revised by L. García y García and G. Panzera).

C.I.J., *Corpus Inscriptionum Judaicarum*. (see under FREY J.-B.).

C.I.L., *Corpus Inscriptionum Latinarum*.

DE FEIS Leopoldo, *Di alcune memorie bibliche scoperte a Pompei*. Atti della Società Colombaria di Firenze dall'anno 1890 al 1900, Firenze 1907, pp. 411-431.

DELLA CORTE, Matteo *Le più remote esplorazioni di Pompei. Nuovi contributi allo studio su Pompei ed i Cristiani*, in Historia, 8, 1934, N. 2, pp. 354-372.

Esplorazioni di Pompei immediatamente successive alla catastrofe dell'anno '79. (Secondo contributo allo studio «Pompei e i Cristiani», In Memoria di Vasile Pârvan, Bucarest 1934, pp. 96-109.

Il criptogramma del «Pater Noster» rinvenuto a Pompei. Rendiconti della Pontificia Accademia Romana di Archeologia Ser. 3 vol. 12 (1936) Roma 1937, pp. 397-400.

Il criptogramma del «Pater Noster». Rendiconti dell'Accad. di Archeol. Lettere e BB.AA. di Napoli N.S. 17, 1937, pp. 79-99.

Pompei ed i Cristiani, Rassegna Stor. Salernitana 3, 1939, pp. 62-69.

I Cristiani a Pompei. Rendiconti dell'Accad. di Archeol. Lettere e BB.AA. di Napoli N.S. 19 (1938-39) Napoli 1939, pp. 3-32.

L'Albergo dei Cristiani a Pompei. Civiltà 3, 1942, n. 9, pp. 73-80.

Fabius Eupor, Princeps Libertinorum, e gli elementi giudaici in Pompei. Atti dell'Accademia Pontaniana N.S. 3 (1949-50) Napoli 1951, pp. 347-353.

Case ed abitanti in Pompei, 2. ed., Pompei – Roma 1954.

DE ROSSI Giovanni Battista, *Una memoria dei Cristiani in Pompei*. Rivista di Archeologia Cristiana 2, 1864, pp. 69-72, 95.

Dei Giudei Libertini e dei Cristiani in Pompei. Rivista di Archeologia Cristiana 2, 1864, pp. 92-93, 95.

Cimitero cristiano di Stabia, Bollettino di Archeologia Cristiana, Ser. 3 vol. 4, 1879, pp. 118-127.

DI CAPUA Francesco, *Le antichità stabiane conservate nella sala capitolare e le origini del Cristianesimo a Stabia*, Caserta (Tip. F. Russo) ca. 1922-24.

FALANGA Lorenzo, *Presenze giudaiche e cristiane a Pompei*. Campania Sacra 11-12 (1980-81) Napoli 1983, pp. 397-402.

FERORELLI N., *Gli Ebrei nell'Italia meridionale dall'età romana al sec. XVIII*. Torino 1915.

FREY Jean-Baptiste, *Les Juifs à Pompéi*. Revue Biblique 42, Paris 1933, pp. 365-384.

*Corpus inscriptionum Iudaicarum. Recueil des inscriptions juives…*1, Città del Vaticano 1936, pp. 408-418. (Abbrev. *C.I.J.*).

GINGSBURG Michael S., *Princeps Libertinorum*. Transanctions Amer. Philol. Assoc. 65, 1934, pp. 198-205.

GIORDANO Carlo - KAHN Isidoro, *Il Cherem biblico in Pompei antica*. Rendiconti dell'Accad. di Archeol. Lettere e BB.AA. di Napoli N.S. 49 (1974) Napoli 1975, pp. 167-176.

GUARDUCCI Margherita, *La più antica iscrizione col nome dei Cristiani*. Römische Quartalschrift 57, 1962, pp. 116-125.

Il misterioso «quadrato magico»: l'interpretazione di Jérôme Carcopino e documenti nuovi. Archeologia classica 17, 1965, pp. 219-270 and *Ancora sul quadrato magico*, ibid, 19, 1967, pp. 144-145.

GUTMANN Joseph, *A Reexamination of the «Judgement of Salomon» Fresco at Pompeii*. Bull. of the Israel Exploration Society 18, 1954, pp. 176-182.

Was there Biblical Art at Pompeii? Antike Kunst 15, Basel 1972, pp. 122-124.

LUMBROSO Giacomo, *Sul dipinto pompeiano in cui si è ravvisato il giudizio di Salomone*. Memorie della R. Accad. dei Lincei, Classe di scienze morali.. Ser. 3 vol. 11 (1882-83) Roma 1883, pp. 303-305.

MAIURI Amedeo, *La croce di Ercolano*. Rendiconti della Pontificia Accademia Romana di Archeologia Ser. 3 vol. 15 (1939) Roma 1940, pp. 193-218.

La Campania al tempo dell'approdo di San Paolo. In: AA.VV. «S. Paolo a Pozzuoli. XIX Centenario», Napoli 1961, pp. 52-75 (The same in: Studi Romani 9, 1961, n. 2, pp. 135-148 and recently new edition, ed. by Domenico Ambrassi, Sorrento – Napoli, F. Di Mauro, 1991).

Sulla datazione del «Quadrato Magico» o Criptogramma cristiano a Pompei. Rendiconti dell'Accad. di Archeol. Lettere e BB.AA. di Napoli N.S.28 (1953), Napoli 1954, pp. 101-111.

MALLARDO Domenico, *La questione dei Cristiani a Pompei*. Rivista di studi pompeiani 1, 1935, Fasc.2 (1934) pp. 116-165 e Fasc.3 (1935) pp. 217-261.

MAULUCCI VIVOLO Francesco Paolo, *Testimonianze giudaiche e cristiane a Pompei prima del 79 d. C.* Tribuna 8, 30 luglio 1983, n. 7, pp. 14-15.

Testimonianze giudaiche e cristiane a Pompei. Il Verbo s'è fermato qui. In: AA.VV. «Salvare Pompei», Napoli ca. 1984, pp. 31-34.

Giudei e Cristiani a Pompei prima del 79. Un inestricabile giallo archeologico. Ulisse, mensile di notizie..., Pompei, marzo-aprile 1989.

E 'acqua zampillerà dal deserto. (Testimonianze giudaiche e cristiane a Pompei prima del 79). Napoli 1990.

NESTLE Eberhard, *Ein Spur des Christentums in Pompeji?.* Zeitschrift für die neu-testamentliche Wissenschaft und die Kunde des Urchristentums 5, 1904, pp. 167-168.

NEWBOLD William Romaine, *Five transliterated Aramaic Inscriptions.* American Journal of Archaeology Ser. 2 vol. 30, 1926, pp. 288-329.

SOGLIANO Antonio, *Di un luogo dei libri Sibillini relativo alla catastrofe delle città campane sepolte dal Vesuvio.* Atti della R. Accad. di Archeol. Lettere e BB.AA. di Napoli 16 (1891-93) Napoli 1894, Parte prima, pp. 165-179.

VARONE Antonio, *Giudei e cristiani nell'area vesuviana.* In: AA.VV. «Pompei 79. XIX Centenario» Supplement to n. 15 of Antiqua, Anno 4, Oct.-Dec. 1979, pp. 131-146.

Presenze giudaiche e cristiane a Pompei. Napoli 1979.

CONTENTS

Finito di stampare nel mese di febbraio 2006
presso la Tipografia Eredi dott. G. Bardi s.r.l. – Roma